Parent Church Landmines

By
Ben Ingebretson
& Tom Nebel

A word about inclusive language:

The authors realize that church planters can be both men and women, but in the interest of readability, have used the pronoun "he" for singular references to church planters.

Published by ChurchSmart Resources

We are an evangelical Christian publisher committed to producing excellent products at affordable prices to help church leaders accomplish effective ministry in the areas of Church planting, Church growth, Church renewal and Leadership development.

For a free catalog of our resources call 1-800-253-4276.
Visit us at: www.ChurchSmart.com

Cover design by: Julie Becker
© Copyright 2009

ISBN: 1-889638-90-0

Table of Contents

Dedication

This book is dedicated to all those parent congregations who, despite their lack of wisdom or coaching, moved ahead in response to their sense of calling and gave birth to a new church. Their experience is our shared wisdom!

Foreword

The American church is facing challenging times. The majority of churches are declining in size and vitality. As the culture of America becomes more postChristian, postmodern, and multiethnic, traditional modes of ministry become less fruitful. Yet there is a bright spot on the horizon. Many Christian leaders are beginning to understand the critical role of planting new churches.

Tom Nebel and Ben Ingebretson have been at the forefront of church planting for a long time. They have pastored, planted, coached and led denominational movements. They have brought energy, vision, insight and humor to everything they do. They both have a boatload of experience in the "how to."

The oft-forgotten 'engine' for a true church planting movement is parent churches. We will never live God's plan for the American church without a greatly increased cohort of churches who believe that one of their purposes is to produce offspring. Parenting is almost always the best and most Biblical way to start a church. If your church is thinking about planting a new church, this book is an invaluable tool to lower your fears, increase your determination, and benefit from its practical advice on how to move forward without stepping on those landmines. And if parenting is a new idea for you, this book will ignite the spark and fan it into flames.

Just as the dynamics of parent-child relationships can be both incredibly fulfilling and amazingly complex, so it is with parenting a new church. Do not proceed without first purchasing this field guide!

I have worked in church planting for 27 years, yet found over a dozen new ideas in this book that are so good that I am going to have to immediately integrate them into how we plant churches. Thanks, Ben and Tom!

David T. Olson
Author of *The American Church in Crisis*.
Executive Minister of Church Growth and Evangelism of the Evangelical Covenant Church.

Introduction

We recently were reminded of what was perhaps the most difficult decade in American history. In the 1930's our nation lived through a colossal meltdown in the financial markets with unemployment reaching over 25%. The sluggish federal response extended the downturn, and many suffered. That was bad enough, but it got worse. Then came the ecological disaster known as the "Dust Bowl" of the American west, depleting lands and leaving farmers and pioneers destitute. It was a result of bad science (it was believed that plowing sod would release rain-producing ions into the atmosphere), poor planning (land overuse) and climatic conditions that were beyond control. The results were "black blizzards" where up to eight or more inches of topsoil went airborne, creating lethal clouds that descended on cities from Des Moines to New York. Livestock by the thousands choked to death on the dust, and people fled for their lives. The 1930's were difficult years, to be sure.

Sometimes extending the Kingdom of God by planting a new church can feel like the 1930s. Parenting a church can be a wonderful experience, resulting in dramatic spiritual and numerical growth for both the parent church and its daughter. It can also become a disaster. For sure, some factors lay beyond our control, and we pray hard when faced with such challenges. "In this world you will have trouble," Jesus said (John 16:33), and planting a new church is bound to produce some adversity. But as stewards of the opportunities and resources before us, we do well to gather information, learn from others, plan well, and step forward in faith. As leaders we want all of our human and material resources to be treated properly. We want to avoid landmines wherever we can.

These are wonderful days of opportunity in the church. Sparked by leading thinkers like Dave Olson (*The American Church in Crisis*) and fueled by most every protestant denomination, there are significant efforts underway to address the decline in church attendance by planting new churches. As we write this introduction, CNN runs a news story about the decline of Christianity in the US. Many of us watch as city center and suburban churches age and stagnate. In spite of these concerns, new churches continue to hold the promise of being best suited to reach new people for Christ. Many of those new churches will be birthed because a parent congregation has caught the vision and is seeking to leave a legacy through church planting. Using a variety of means and methods, these parent churches will put their values into action. Some will multi-site, others will host a new start on their campus, still others will offer a planter a "fishing license" to take who they can into a new venture of faith.

Parent Church Landmines is intended to serve the churches that have heard the call to help birth the next generation of new churches in America. It is borne from many years and many experiences on the front lines, shoulder to shoulder with pastors and ministry leaders who are giving their all to birth a new church. They are the ones who have done the field work that gives this book whatever credibility it has. This work represents a price that has been paid in setbacks and detours along the way — and it hopes to rescue many from repeating the mistakes of the past. It is a companion volume to the earlier book, *Church Planting Landmines* (Tom Nebel and Gary Rohrmayer, 2005), and looks at church planting pitfalls from the perspective of the parent church. Both books seek to help steward the pioneer energy that is being invested in church planting today.

Our experience is that some of the best churches are never born, because the parent churches who could reproduce fail to pick up the pieces and plant again, especially when they've had a bad experience. *Parent Church Landmines* seeks to help embolden the planting of new churches, whether this is a first-time or repeat experience for the parent congregation. Each chapter describes a common landmine, reinforcing the teaching with stories to bring the reader beyond sterile theory. These ministry concussions have actually taken place!

Peter Wagner put it memorably when he said, "Birthing rooms are almost always bloody places." Understanding this, we offer helpful tools and insights to aid in safer birthing. No two church plants are identical, so our desire is to prescribe principles and offer experiences for you to apply to your particular setting. Included are several helpful appendices that can take you deeper in gaining insight and direction. Together our hope is that these lessons will equip your ministry to reproduce well – again and again.

Ben Ingebretson
Grand Rapids, Michigan

Tom Nebel
Madison, Wisconsin

Chapter 1

Paralyzing Fear

"To live in a fully predictable world is not to be human" C.S.Lewis

When talking about parenting a new church, it is too easy to do just that! Some years ago the region I served played host to a church planting conference. With over 180 congregations, including many large ones with untapped parenting potential, I hoped for some significant church planting results. We arranged for a nationally known proponent of church planting to come, and we marketed the event to hundreds. The event came and went with all the fanfare and participation I had hoped for. I recall at one point the presenter was asked, "How large must our church be before we give birth?" After a long pause he shocked the crowd of pastors by saying, "Fifty people". He went on to make the point that the larger a church becomes and the more sophisticated their leadership, the lower the chances are that they will ever parent. I was skeptical of his response then, but I am no more.

Six years later most of the congregations that attended our event still have not parented a new church. It seems they have gone through "ready, aim…." but cannot pull the trigger and "fire!". In fact, it seems the conversation has dropped entirely off their radar screen! Meanwhile, other congregations, both large and small, have moved forward in birthing new churches with considerable success and fruitfulness. Why is it that some churches say they believe in church planting, yet never actually do it?

FEAR FACTOR

Have you ever stopped to consider the power of fear? A number of years ago Dale Carnegie wrote the book *How To Stop Worrying and Start Living*. The title says it all. Fear and worry can snuff the life out of a person, a relationship and even a church! Congregations that insist they play ministry in the "no risk zone" are likely to accomplish very little for the Kingdom.

Nevertheless, fear is the predictable first emotional reaction to the idea of a church reproducing itself. Understand I said, *emotional* reaction. More likely you will hear questions about a great many other issues and concerns that are more appropriate in the "planning" or "execution" phase of a new church. Fair enough, people will have questions, and that's a good thing. But even when those questions are answered logically and completely, the pushback will often betray the deep fears that are brewing in the minds of the congregation.

Planting a new church will "sift" the leadership of a church. It will expose your deepest beliefs and non-beliefs, and in so doing, it will reveal fears. Here are some of the more common fears I have encountered in my experience:

- Fear that we will lose our best leadership people to the new plant.
- Fear that we will be financially crippled by the cost of planting.
- Fear that the new plant will struggle and reflect poorly on the parent.
- Fear that another preacher will outshine ours.
- Fear that some of our best friends will go with the new plant.
- Fear that the experience will push our leadership beyond their time and abilities.
- Fear that the new congregation will stray from our convictions.
- Fear that in some way the new church will diminish us.

This is not a comprehensive list. But I think I can comfortably say that whatever the fear is, the sooner the leadership of a ministry can identify and address it, the sooner things will begin moving forward. Most people will simply not be persuaded to "do the right thing" if that persuasion does not address what they are feeling in the deepest recesses of their hearts. It is at this level that our great adversary wants to paralyze us with fear while the Bible consistently beckons us forward with the admonition to "fear not." I have never seen this fundamental battle won apart from the commitment of the key leaders and their team to move past fear. Perhaps the greatest fear is the "scorecard fear." If parenting a new church negatively impacts our ministry scorecard, we pull back. For this reason, we need to take another look at how we measure ministry.

SCORECARD FEARS

"Who is keeping score?" It's a question we ask in a lot of settings and a question worthy of parenting churches. Sometimes we don't keep score the same way

God keeps score. When sizing up churches, for instance, we often ask: How big is it? How many attendees does it have? or What is their facility like? In denominational circles, it's not uncommon to champion only the bright and beautiful churches. It is their pastors who speak at our conferences and are highlighted in our publications. People count, so numbers count, but by keeping score only in attendance figures, we may fail to acknowledge the number of new congregations started by a parent as they release people to "seed" a new church! Times are changing, and ministry scorecards should be changing too.

In the denomination I serve, we are watching our scorecard change. This change is challenging some long-held assumptions and patterns. We still get excited when we hear about great things happening at our large churches. We still get excited when we hear of any church that's growing. But we're also thrilled when we hear of churches that are multiplying themselves. Collectively we have adopted a ten-year goal to plant 400 churches across America. It's a goal that is shaking some lazy and complacent habits. Recently, at a meeting of church planting leaders who evaluated our progress at year five, we recognized that in order to achieve our dream we would need to double our number of parent congregations. That means a lot of congregations will have to conquer their fears of releasing new people to start a new ministry. We need to champion the role of parent churches in our overall church planting mission. Our scorecard has to change.

Today we work hard to tell the stories and lift up the examples of churches that start churches. Little-by-little our culture is changing as we seek to measure success by multiplying, birthing and parenting. It excites me that this year alone several of our young churches (younger than five years old) are actively taking steps to birth daughter churches. "Birthing before building" is becoming a familiar mantra, and our hope is that by championing parent churches more and more we will "spur one another on ..." (Hebrews 10:24). A new scorecard is coming into focus, rooted in the gospel call to give, send and release. Old fears associated with attendance decline are being replaced by the affirmation of a parent who sends people into the harvest!

OBJECTION!

There are a number of reasons to object to the premise that all churches can participate in parenting new churches. Some churches seem too small. Some churches need to get to the "next level" before they're ready to actively encourage people to move out into a new venture with a new leader. Maybe so. But one interesting response is told by Charles Arn in his book, *How To Start A Second Service*. While the act of starting a second worship service is not the same as starting a new church, it does bear enough similarity to make a point. One church, Westminster Presbyterian of Duluth, MN, had about forty people in worship when they decided to multiply. They decided to multiply because they were small. Remarkably, within twenty-four months, the church grew to over 200 people! An act of faith, based on the fact that stagnation was occurring, resulted in a five-fold increase in the church. Planting a new church pushes stagnant churches into new paradigms. It removes much of the programming and thinking that has proven itself ineffective, creating a clean slate with a top priority to reach new people.

I love the story of Bob, a retired man who now looks back on his life as a key lay person. At one time, Bob left his role as an elder in a parent church to serve with the daughter church for a number of years. He served in ways he had never imagined and was stretched in ways that expanded his faith. In his retirement years, he resettled back to his original church. There, over time, Bob was agitating for the church to birth a new ministry again. At one point he stood before the membership and told his story, reporting that it was church planting that grew him like no other experience in ministry. Today one of Bob's sons and his family are active in the start of a new church!

THE LEAD-OFF PASTOR

In baseball, the lead-off batter is the spark for the rest of the lineup. What he does sets the pace for those who follow. In parenting a new church, the lead-off role belongs to the lead communicator and senior pastor, who must address and move beyond his or her personal fears before imparting courage to others. Gaining courage can be a private quest, or it can take place in a network of other pastors who gather to provide mutual learning, support and accountability. The speed of the leader will determine the speed of the congregation!

The challenges and fears of a local congregation can easily take the eye of the senior leader off the goal, consuming him with routine responsibilities and crises. A network of pastors can provide the environment for learning, support and accountability. One such group that meets in my region takes a rotating "case study" approach to their time with each participant reporting their action steps from the last month. Together these leaders move ahead with the benefits of shared wisdom and collegial support. There may be no better way to help local leaders press past the resistance they encounter because of fear. With a regular support and accountability group, leaders sense that they are not alone in new territory.

Growing conviction, wisdom, support and accountability in the senior leader raise the potential that the congregation will catch the bold dream of reproducing itself. It all starts when the pastor "leads off," going public with the congregational leadership to outline the faith dream. This vision can be communicated through a variety of means including:

- Preaching and teaching the book of Acts to make the biblical case.
- Interviewing a church planter in your area.
- Telling the stories of church plants in your area.
- Identifying unreached people groups near you with a map in the foyer.
- Sharing denominational church planting goals.
- Promoting a book to read on church planting.
- Interviewing the founding members of your, or another, congregation.
- Teaching on planting through small groups and adult classes.

Promotion is a key role of leadership. People make time and give energy to what they consider to be important. It is the role of the leader to define "important" and then channel that time and energy toward the goal. Promotion takes time as the pastor seeks the buy-in of the elders and other senior leaders, followed by the endorsement of the church at large. Because planting will involve a significant commitment on the part of the parent church in time, prayer, finances and people, it is important that promotion touches the formal leaders and the opinion leaders of the ministry. At any point along the way, leadership is likely to face opposition. Parenting a new church can be a significant redirection for a congregation, and change always creates its own set of challenges and unintended consequences.

MOVING PAST FEAR OF CHANGE

There is no change without discomfort and resistance. Change creates pushback, and the change that involves church planting is no different. Early on, leaders who propose to plant are likely to experience the "20-50-30" principle. That is, 20 percent will love the new vision, 50 percent will be neutral, and 30 percent will resist you. Don't make the mistake of expecting to have the complete support of every member as you move forward. It is very unlikely that everyone will get on board for the critical issues of your ministry. Some folks simply remain resisters!

Capturing the commitments of your key leaders and a majority of your congregation is vital in order to bring about change.

John Kotter in his book *Leading Change* (HBS Press 1996) outlines some principles for change tactics that are very helpful.

- Create a sense of urgency with stories and statistics. Make the case.
- Explain your reasoning often and with multiple means. Over-communicate.
- Vigorously teach and preach biblical values that support planting.
- Develop a guiding coalition including people with credibility, expertise, leadership gifts and positional power.
- Promise problems. Setbacks are part of progress.
- Go public with your deep commitment. People are watching you closely.
- Respectfully get to the heart of the resisters and answer them.
- Reward the behaviors you desire. Positive reinforcement creates incentive.
- Set the pace with a proposed timeline for the project.

Recently I met with a pastor whose church was thinking about parenting a new church. He admitted that there were resisters to this vision. This church had just completed a major building project when a key young leader rose up and announced his having been called to plant a church. Together we agreed that the resisters to this young new planter and his vision had some validity in their concerns. After all, the paint was not yet dry on their new construction! I have had many similar conversations and have come to agree with the saying, "There is never a perfect time to plant a new church." We can always find a significant reason not to. The budget is strained, we just committed to a new missionary, or the congregation just needs some time to "settle in". Moving past these subtle resisters will only take place when the deep biblical values of mission and outreach are held out as imperatives and people are challenged to rise up-- and measure up.

THE PROCESS IS THE PRODUCT

Sometimes significant fear and resistance come from expecting people to swallow too much at once. Planting is a process that can be broken down into little steps. Often times leadership teams agonize over planting, feeling that they must have answers to every detail before they vote the plant forward. An alternative approach is to move ahead as far as is reasonably possible and then wait for a clear signal before the next major step forward. I think of these steps as "triggers." For example:

1. The first trigger is the buy-in of the senior leader. Until the pastor is "all in" the plant cannot move ahead.

2. The second trigger is the church board. Until they are "all in" the plant cannot move ahead.
3. The third trigger is a movement of prayer. Until the congregation takes the spiritual reality seriously and begins to pray, the plant cannot move ahead.
4. The fourth trigger may be a planning team which guides the general process.
5. The fifth trigger could be a preliminary plan, including target audience, budget, and planting model.
6. The sixth trigger may be the selection of the right planter and coach.
7. The seventh trigger may be the raising of funds.
8. The final trigger may be the agreement of the planting plan and hiring a planter.

The process approach opens the possibility that at any point the plant could stop if a "trigger" is not released.   Be health-driven, not calendar-driven.   This raises the likelihood of due diligence in every step of the way, reducing fear and increasing faith for the parent church.

PENCIL PLANNING YOUR WAY PAST FEAR

I often sit with church board leadership teams who are exploring church planting and are dealing with a fundamental conflict. Some of them (usually the engineers, doctors and teachers) want all the answers and planning on paper first while the rest of them (the business people and human service workers) are content to take things one step at a time. Most teams address a fear tension by developing an exhaustive plan which can be helpful. However, the number one variable in any church plant is the planter. His age, affinity and background will likely determine with whom he will be most effective. If you are not certain as to your planter, it is important that you hold the details of your plan lightly. Plan in pencil.

Extending a call to a planter is the single most critical decision you will make in parenting. To help that person discern the "rightness of fit" with your congregation you are wise to lay out a preliminary planting plan. That plan should encompass three major areas.

1. The target audience.

Who do you believe God is calling you to reach in a new way? These could be people who are culturally distant but geographically close (or they may be geographically distant but culturally close). There is no single right answer for all churches, but there is likely a best target for your church. Demographic research can often be a source of insight in making this decision. Perhaps a look at your own congregation will give you a strong hint. If you are effective in reaching a particular age group, then you may be able to continue that effort in a new location. Ultimately, however, your planter will determine the answer to your target. You must seek a planter who can forge a strong affinity relationship with a potential target group.

2. The planting method.

Church planting is more of an art than a science. The call to "bear much fruit" can take place through many different means. Your particular target and the giftedness of the church planter will shed light on the most appropriate method you should choose. The key is to write your preliminary plan in pencil. Be open to changes along the way, and be aware that God will be leading in the heart of your church planter. You can pencil in a probable method, but over time, that method may change. After all, our commitment is to reach the harvest, not to run a model.

3. The financial plan

Most prospective parent churches immediately gravitate to the issue of finances when determining their planting plan. That's fine. Finances will dictate a lot, but finances will not dictate everything. At the end of the day, vision trumps finances. Outlining the sources, amounts, and extent of financial commitment is important. There are the budgetary factors of salary, facilities, equipment, and operations. Still, you may be surprised at how the picture changes in light of the right planter. Some planters put a high priority on being bi-vocational in the early season of their plant to build relationships with outsiders. Other planters will raise significant funds from family, friends, and churches. These two variables alone can stretch the time needed for the new congregation to become self-sustaining. Your budget is best outlined in pencil until you have a planter. By taking these significant first steps of discovering the target audience, determining the best methods and developing a financial plan (all in pencil) you will have done your new church planter a real service.

PRAYING FORWARD

Scripture reminds us to fight fear with prayer (Phil. 4:6). The great prayer teacher E.M. Bounds put it this way; "Prayer is not preparation for the battle, prayer is the battle." If you can get your leaders and congregation praying about church planting you will be surprised how the energy and focus align. Prayer changes things, and the first thing it changes is us!

The challenge is getting people to pray. Before that, however, is the challenge of getting myself to pray. If your church wants to parent a new church, the lead-off batter for the prayer movement should be the senior leader. There is no better time for a prayer retreat and prayer focus than the time you are sensing the earliest inklings from God to parent a new congregation. The saying, "speed of the leader is the speed of the team," is particularly true when it comes to prayer. When the senior leader has a protracted time in prayer resulting in a cultivated soul in accord with God's vision, the result will be evident to others. Prayer is powerful in how it syncs us into God's values. When a prayer leader calls the community to account before God, there is an impact that reverberates throughout the congregation.

Some years back I developed and reproduced a simple 3x5 card with this inscription: *"Pray the Lord of the harvest to raise up a new church planter in 2005."* It was a very biblical prayer (from Matthew 9:37) tied to the year of ministry vision we had claimed for a new plant. People posted the attractive call to prayer on their bathroom mirrors and refrigerators and a movement of prayer began. Other prayer strategies I have experienced include:

- Prayerwalking the neighborhoods near a new plant
- Including planting in your weekly "pastoral prayer"
- Creating an email prayer loop for weekly updates and planting prayer
- Asking for names of people in the area, and begining to pray for them
- Developing an intercessor team for your planter … known or unknown

Recently we watched again the power of prayer in planting as we asked several congregations to pray about a new plant about 20-30 miles from them. To our great joy and wonder we watched as the call to prayer drew out resources and interest in the plant. In a few months we had nearly fifty new leads of interested people and prospects for the core group. At the same time we listened to hear how the congregations surrounding the plant had been challenged to think about parenting themselves. With that groundswell of support, the parent congregation was greatly encouraged to move past fear. Prayer in planting is job one!

Questions to consider while navigating the landmine of Paralyzing Fear:

- What are the spoken fears that surround church planting in your congregation?
- What are the unspoken fears that surround church planting in your congregation?
- Does your leadership team include a balance of those with the gift of faith and those with gifts of wisdom and discernment?
- How will you gain the endorsement of the opinion leaders?

Recommended Resources:

- *Five Things Anyone Can Do to Help Start a Church* by Phil Stevenson, Wesleyan Publishing House, 2008
- *Resistance: Moving Beyond Barriers to Change* by Price Pritchett, Pritchett, LP
- *Leading Change* by John Kotter, Harvard Business School Press, 1996

Chapter 2

Values Disconnect

"If you want to know if a person is religious don't ask, just observe."
— Ludwig Wittgenstein

Here is a story that can likely be retold too many times. A leadership board of a local church came to a crossroads, recognizing that if they didn't start a new worship service they would continue to lose their younger families. Though seated around a table, they felt like their backs were against a wall. For years they had touted their "stake in the ground"-- a commitment to a "historic worship" style. Now a series of exit interviews plus a groundswell of lobbying by younger members had forced a reconsideration of their position. Other churches in the denomination were "going missional" and placing higher value on "the people not here yet." Foreign mission ("the ends of the earth") had always been important, so now the elders reasoned it was time to take that missional value and bring it home (to "Jerusalem and Judea"). They would start a contemporary outreach service! This met well with the outreach team who had been pushing for the church to be more outwardly focused for a long time.

In time, staffing changes and new instrumentalists seemed to set the stage for a second, more contemporary, service to "close the back door" on those young families. But now they were faced with what was a deal breaker issue and they agonized late into the night over this new crossroad. The problem was with the timing of the second service. The elders agreed that the traditional service would not move from the 10:00 a.m. slot. Any earlier, and people would have to rush their Sunday morning preparations. And later would cramp coffee and education which immediately followed. So the best option was to hold the "outreach service" at 11:30. No sooner had the elders announced this, however, than a new wave of protest emerged. The 11:30 a.m. worship slot was not appreciated by those who were on the outreach team. They challenged the elders, wondering how they could expect outsiders to "try out church" with a worship service at such an inconvenient hour. As they saw things, the worship schedule was entirely self-serving, with the unchurched of the community getting the leftovers.

A defining value in their ministry had been illuminated. And in a single decision the leadership trumpeted that core value to the congregation and community.

VALUES REAL AND PERCEIVED

Pick a set of values, any set you like, and you have to question its authenticity. Suppose I claim to value mom, America and apple pie. Then Mother's Day comes around and I fail to send a card and flowers. I cheat on my taxes, and I buy cherry pie every year at the county fair. The question could genuinely be raised as to the authenticity of my values.

Values can easily be perceived to be real by individuals or organizations as a result of any one of several contributing factors. Take history, for example. Somewhere in my past you can probably find evidence to support the notion that I value Brussels sprouts. But you may have to go a long way back and settle for very little evidence. Or how about appearances? It may look like I am really listening to you, but my actual thoughts are a million miles away. Consider an inflated ego. We can actually think and talk ourselves into a distorted self-concept. Most adolescents imagine themselves invincible until there is a bump with reality. The point is this: values can be tricky, and the tricks they play are most often on ourselves. Sometimes those closest to us can discern the difference between what is real and what is veneer. A close friend knows that just because I ate Brussels sprout puree as an infant, I'm not necessarily a Brussels sprouts enthusiast today. So values are tricky. Casual observers may miss our true values, and we might deceive ourselves as well.

Congregations get into trouble when they rest on thin evidence of the past, or on flimsy window dressing appearances, as the witness to their values. Values should have recent and frequent evidence that demonstrate their reality. Otherwise they are merely perceived to be so. The story of the church leadership team and the time slot of an outreach service is an example of the problem. Call the desire to reach lost people an ideal or a goal, but don't call it a value until there is evidence to prove it!

TWO CHURCHES....TWO SETS OF VALUES

Often Christians think romantically about the early days of the church—the "first century church"—as if there was an ideal template which we are to aspire toward. The truth is, however, that even in the earliest days local churches expressed different values and different emphases. Consider these two "first churches" and the striking differences between them. They are each the "first church" of a certain kind!

First Church Jerusalem

The Jerusalem church is the first congregational model that Luke describes in Acts 2:42 and Acts 15:1-4. Anchored in the Jewish community and its practice (as well as the apostolic witness of the earliest followers of Christ), this church evidenced particular historical values. For starters, this community valued the tradition that had been handed down to them. The early Christians in Jerusalem, as Jewish followers of Jesus, centered their experience in the synagogue and temple, where Jesus himself would have taught and worshiped. These institutions were rich in symbolism, history, and tradition. With the message of the resurrected Christ, early believers would have expected to transform the synagogue and temple into the structure of the church rather than to start another competing spiritual community. While that possibility diminished, the values of history and tradition were passed on to the first believers.

The Jerusalem church was also theologically sophisticated, given the fact that believers came out of a Jewish system of education and religious practice. Much of Jesus' message was understood in light of the prophetic foreshadowing found in the Hebrew Scriptures. Imagine sermons from Leviticus that everyone understood! In this context, anything less than significant theological depth and sophistication would not have been "seeker sensitive." In addition, the Jerusalem church was culturally homogenous, with nearly everyone sharing a taste for the same ethnic foods and traditions during holy days. The first church of Jerusalem would have embraced its cultural roots and heritage.

Later, in Acts 15, we get a glimpse of a unique episode in the history of the Jerusalem church that surfaces another value. The question arose, especially on the edge of the expanding church, whether Gentiles had to first become Jews before they could become Christians. At issue was the unsettling question of whether male circumcision was required as a rite into the church. So the question came back to the Jerusalem leadership (Acts 15:2) which was anchored in the apostolic leaders. Their response (which did not require circumcision for the

Gentiles), gives evidence to the value they placed on the authority of their leaders. The apostles had remained there from the dramatic days of Holy Week until the day of Pentecost. Leadership and location were fused together by events that shook the world!

History, tradition, theological depth, cultural homogeneity, and solidified leadership were the overarching values for the privileged people of the covenant. This church was remarkable in being suited to reach and keep the people who were closest to them. Their values supported their action and their action reinforced their values.

First Church Antioch

The Antioch Church is recorded for us in Acts 11:19-26 and Acts 13:1-3. It was a church born from dispersion and persecution, and it wasn't nearly as culturally homogeneous as the church in Jerusalem. In fact, this church intentionally sought to convert Greeks to faith in Christ.

> "[19]Now those who had been scattered by the persecution in connection with Stephen traveled as far as Phoenicia, Cyprus and Antioch, telling the message only to Jews. [20]Some of them, however, men from Cyprus and Cyrene, went to Antioch and began to speak to Greeks also, telling them the good news about the Lord Jesus. [21]The Lord's hand was with them, and a great number of people believed and turned to the Lord. (Acts 11:19-21)

The leadership of this church was also culturally diverse, and, consequently, they were hard-wired for mission. For them, the gospel was for the world, not just for the people of the Covenant.

> [1]In the church at Antioch there were prophets and teachers: Barnabas, Simeon called Niger, Lucius of Cyrene, Manaen (who had been brought up with Herod the tetrarch) and Saul. [2]While they were worshiping the Lord and fasting, the Holy Spirit said, "Set apart for me Barnabas and Saul for the work to which I have called them." [3]So after they had fasted and prayed, they placed their hands on them and sent them off. (Acts 13:1-3)

It wasn't easy to be Christians anywhere in the first century, but while the church in Jerusalem enjoyed relative peace and comfort, the Antioch believers were welded together by fire and adversity. They had shared struggles and pain. The effect of that experience was to shake loose some previously held practices and values, preparing them to embrace the vast new opportunities to come.

Instead of seeking those who had a common ethnic background, this rag tag group was ethnically and culturally diverse. The message was no longer for Jews only. Creativity and contextualization ruled the day for the church in Antioch. Imagine the experiment in communication that they undertook as they learned to contextualize the gospel message to non-Jews. Luke summarizes their message as "the good news about the Lord Jesus" (vs.20), now available to Jew and Gentile alike.

Reading the account of First Church Antioch we note the values of creativity, diversity and theological simplicity. That's quite a contrast with the First Church Jerusalem and the values that arose from that context. Later, Luke describes the commissioning of new leaders in Barnabas and Saul (later known as Paul), an expression of empowering others for leadership to disseminate the Gospel. Accordingly, Antioch seems to have placed a higher overall value on mission to outsiders while Jerusalem placed greater value on ministering within the culture.

These two churches are certainly a study in contrasts, but more than that, they also seem to exemplify a progression in God's expanding design for ministry. Over time, the Jerusalem church becomes a distant, antiquated voice in the unfolding drama of mission, while the Antioch church catalyzed mission around the Mediterranean basin. We're prompted to ask this question: Of the two early churches, which value system does my church more closely reflect?

Jerusalem Values	Antioch Values
1. Historic and faithful	1. Creative and pragmatic
2. Culturally homogenous	2. Culturally diverse
3. Solidified leadership	3. Expanding leadership
4. Gate-keeping authority	4. Permission-giving authority
5. Theologically developed	5. Theologically simple
6. Focused on the privileged people	6. Focused on the outsiders

VALUES THAT DRIVE MISSIONAL CHURCHES

Here are Logan and Ogne's seven common values of congregations that reproduce:

- Compassion for the unchurched – Caring enough about lost people that significant amounts of time are invested in reaching them.

- Culturally relevant style – Utilize a style of ministry that attracts seekers and addresses their needs.
- Great commission orientation – See ministry potential in terms of people who need to be reached rather than in terms of financial or facility limitations.
- Developing and releasing leaders – Actively seeks to give away best leaders to start new churches.
- Confidence in God's ability – Makes bold plans with faith in God's resources.
- Kingdom perspective – Encourages new churches to start close to home while also looking at the world-wide harvest.
- Generosity – Giving freely of people and finances to start new churches.

(*Churches Planting Churches* by Robert E. Logan and Steven L. Ogne Published by ChurchSmart Resources, 1995. p. 3-5)

In many ways this list parallels the first church at Antioch. While the first church at Jerusalem likely would one day reproduce itself, the church at Antioch was hard-wired from the beginning to be an outreach-oriented church planting church. To assess the presence of these values in your church, see Appendix A "Preparing to Parent Values Assessment" at the back of this book.

A couple of years ago I had a conversation with Ken, who was a seasoned pastor serving a church for many years. Under his leadership, Ken had seen the church grow by adding two weekend services. As I explored that experience with him, I asked where the resistance came when they began to expand. He reported the predictable issues; some were upset that they would not see all their old friends together any more, others that there were not enough musicians, still others that it was inconvenient and messy. When I asked Ken how he handled those objections his answer was "preaching and teaching." Ken said that prior to each successful launch of a new weekend service he worked hard to preach and teach the core values that drove the ministry.

"Convenience" and "seeing all your friends" simply were not on the biblical list of values that drove the ministry. Ken fully leveraged his communication opportunities to spotlight missional values, and when it came time to implement change, the right things happened.

As leaders we are wise to remember that the river never flows higher than its source. If we are to lead a church to become a church-planting church, we must be examples in our own lives of the values that we long to see demonstrated in our church. Each of the seven values in Logan and Ogne's list can be manifested personally in our lives. We must be the change we long to see in our church. Some time ago I recall wishing my church was more empowering of leaders. Then it dawned on me that I had not been training someone to replace me in some of my duties, and the result was to limit the growth of others. I had to change! This is the beginning of congregational renewal. It begins with me and my obedience to God.

THREE EXERCISES TO MOVE AHEAD

Reflecting on the multiplication values list is likely to generate a reaction in most of us. Some immediately resonate with these as consistent with who they are. Others may not. The first exercise is to explore this list with a group of leaders. Take them one at a time and ask "How is this value fueling missional energy at our church?" This general overview can help the leadership gain appreciation for how each value is or is not contributing to a congregation that is outwardly focused and missionally engaged.

For the second exercise, assign a numerical score to each missional value. Take each value and give it a rating of 1-10, with a 1 indicating a PERCEIVED VALUE and a 10 indicating a REAL VALUE in your church.

1. Compassion for those far from God

1_____10

Perceived Value   Real Value

(little or no evidence to prove it)   (significant evidence to prove it)

2. Culturally relevant style

1_____10

Perceived Value   Real Value

This may take some time as people on your team have different impressions of the ministry because of varying degrees of exposure to it. Beware of the "halo effect," where one tends to give oneself higher rankings than he deserves. Take the group average for each rating to arrive at a score for each value. Ranking the seven multiplication values is an important step and will give priority to your work.

For the third exercise, take your lowest multiplication value rating and work to improve it by developing an action plan. Then implement that action plan! Consider the following example:

1. *Compassion for those far from God* score: 3

Action Plan: Beginning immediately, two Sundays every month will include public prayer for the lost.

> Seek out those with the gift of evangelism and invite them to share their stories with the church.   Start with one each week for the first month, with one per month following.   Staff members will each seek to develop one new relationship with an unchurched person.

There are times when a church is presented with a cluster of low scores that can be overwhelming.   The good news is that the seven multiplication values are tethered to each other, and they tend to move up and down as a group.   That means, for example, that if you choose to work on elevating the value of developing and releasing leaders, you are also likely to have a positive impact on other values such as confidence in God's provision, having a Great Commission orientation, possessing compassion for those far from God, and so on.   Be encouraged. Progress may come sooner than you think!

FIVE SPARK IDEAS TO GET STARTED

Phil Stevenson, in his book *Five Things Anyone Can Do To Help Start a Church* has provided a great resource to help pastors break the inertia that holds back taking concrete steps toward church planting.   His five suggestions are:

- **Go public** with your personal passion for church planting.   Make space for God to deepen your passion through prayer and reflection, and then share that with others.
- **Draw others into prayer for lost people**.   Prayer walks, prayer for area church plants, regular mention in Sunday worship prayer, or creating a prayer calendar can direct focus.
- **Promote the concept** through a special Sunday, preaching on New Testament planting stories, a map highlighting area plants or telling the story of how your church was planted.
- **Practice generosity** toward new church start efforts around you.   Send a team to volunteer, begin to budget toward your future plant, throw a shower for a baby church.

- **Give permission** for your people to dream, pray and leave to participate in a new church start. This is a bold move that will stir up energy beyond your imagination!

PARENTING, DNA AND MULTIPLICATION VALUES

America needs more than the addition of a few thousand churches to keep up with its population growth. Dave Olsen, author of *The American Church in Crisis,* predicts 55,000 churches will close between 2005 and 2020 while only 60,000 will open. That gain of 4,500 churches will be a long way from the 48,000 required to keep up with population growth. We need a multiplication movement beyond what we have seen in recent years. That will only take place when churches plant churches which, in turn, plant more churches. Is this possible? Only if there is a return to the values of the Antioch church. Prospective parent congregations must plow these values deeply into their ministry soil, pushing back any subtle leanings toward self-centeredness and privilege. Biblical values are the foundation upon which a church planting system can be built. From that base emerges vision, leadership and resources.

This year I celebrated my 50th birthday. Grim news for some, but not for me! I'm actually optimistic about this benchmark, because my parents both lived into their 90's. I have inherited precious good DNA from them, giving me a genetic predisposition toward a long life. It's no guarantee that I'll live long, but it does give me a good running start.

Similarly, churches who plant churches will pass on their genetic composition to their offspring. As stewards of the churches for which they are responsible, good leaders will perform genetic engineering when the opportunity presents itself. They will take a good look at their values and do what is necessary to correct them. Developing biblical multiplication values in a parent church will pay dividends both now and in the future. Those values will be passed on, like DNA, through stories, experiences, and changed lives for generations to come.

Questions to consider while navigating the landmine of Values Disconnect:

- When was the last time you took a close look at your "real" values?
- Who has responsibility to lead the "values culture" in your congregation?
- What are the next steps for you in connecting biblical values to a planting dream?

Recommended Resources:
- *The Celtic Way of Evangelism* by George Hunger, Abingdon 2000
- *Fragile Hope* by Tom Bandy, Abingdon Press 2002
- *Preparing to Parent* Congregational Assessment Tool (Appendix A)
- *Breaking the Missional Code* by Ed Stetzer and David Putman, Broadman & Holman 2006

Chapter 3

Lack of Trust and Accountability

Whether you're on a sports team, in an office or a member of a family,
if you can't trust one another there's going to be trouble.
— Joe Paterno

I was seated in a coffee shop with a church planter and together we wondered where things had gone wrong. The project started with so much optimism and vigor. A daughter church emerging from a parent congregation that was not yet five years old herself! The mother church was full of hope for their first "kid." Now the planter had been on the field for just over a year and already there was a cloud over the project.

The story really began with the enthusiasm of a young congregation to birth a new church. It was unprecedented to see a church this young (the mother church did not even have its own building yet) launch a new church. The lead pastor, however, was confident that this was the right time to multiply and, along with his team, worked hard to develop a careful plan. Things moved into gear, and a planter was hired.

Within six months of arriving on the scene, the planter began to identify problems in the plan he had inherited from the parent. For starters, he fundamentally disagreed with the location of the project. His read of the situation called for the plant target to move several miles in another direction and take an approach considerably different than the seeker-oriented style of the parent. Months passed by, during which the planter and parent were in different worlds of perception and intent. The planter busied himself with developing a grass roots movement of core people who shared his perspective. As time passed, the planter grew in conviction that his changing agenda was appropriate. Then came the collision.

Being accountable to a denominational system which had money in the project, the planter was approached with a summons to an Oversight Team meeting. A local leader would be chairing the discussion, and an agenda had been prepared. In that meeting the planter suddenly recognized that he had been put in a defensive position. Questions came, and the team asked for reports. The planter disclosed his divergent perspective, and the feeling in the room tightened. Seeing that the original intent of the plant was being violated, the outside leadership team closed ranks and took control. Three such meetings later, the planter and I sat drinking coffee. It was not a fun conversation.

GOOD INTENTIONS

Every parent, at some point, wants the best for his or her kids. We want them to be well-fed and cared for when they are young ... to have the best opportunities as they begin school … to enjoy the things we have found most likeable and satisfying … and ultimately to embrace our outlook on life and the world. These things we do in relationship with our kids are motivated by love and the very best intentions. We reason that we are wiser and will be held responsible for the result. And at times, if we are honest, we also are aware that others are looking and we want our child to reflect well on us. It's the truth!

So many of the dynamics that impact biological parenting also impact spiritual parenting. Mature congregations that feel called to birth a new church want everything to be optimal for their offspring. They form teams that do a lot of study and preparation before hiring a church planter. I consulted with one mother church that had selected the new church name, worship style, location and had even recruited the praise team before hiring a planter. All they needed was to "plug in" a pastor and the picture would be perfectly complete! It's not until later adolescence that parents might discover that all that control just may backfire dramatically.

Parenting a new church is not a cookie-cutter proposition. There are dozens of variables. In some cases the parent may be able to reasonably predict and script many of the best decisions from inception to launch, and an internally grown leader may fit hand-in-glove. In many other cases, especially when the church planter is an unknown, the script will be much less predictable. If the parent church has done its due diligence, it will hire a planter who is gifted enough and smart enough to lead the new church well. That same person will naturally want to lead his team through the thinking and reasoning of many of the design decisions of the plant. After all, they are the ones who have to live with the outcomes every Monday morning. For anyone to survive and thrive in the often draining work of church planting, they have to feel the ministry has their fingerprints on it. Like the small business owner who arrives early and stays late, the planter must be deeply invested in the core identity of the new church dream.

MAMMALS AND REPTILES

One helpful metaphor to consider in parenting a new church comes to us from the animal kingdom. If you think about it, there are different ways in which newborns are parented into the world! Take sea turtles for example. A giant female leatherback will leave dozens of fertilized eggs buried in the sand on a coastal beach. When she is finished delivering, she slips back into the water as an empty nester! The little leatherbacks will hatch one by one and make a scramble from their sandy nursery for the nourishing water that will become their home. But not so fast. First they will face the seagulls who will pick off some as easy lunch. Those who do make it to the water will still face the fierce predators of the sea. In the end, only a small portion of the baby leatherbacks will survive. Many, probably most, will die. Reptiles tend to bear many young and depend on the law of averages to ensure that some will survive.

Mammals tend to take a very different approach to birthing. Take a cow, for instance. When she gives birth to her calf she surrounds her with a great deal of care and nurturing. All that licking and nuzzling is an investment in one life. The mother dutifully nurses her calf until it is able to eat. If threatened, she will defend it. In most cases, she will see her one calf survive until adulthood.

Some church planting is like reptilian birthing. The parent accepts the fact that there will be a high mortality rate but that the law of averages will produce some survivors. Perhaps you know of a church planter who received a very modest stipend and a generous prayer before being thrust out of the nest to plant. Good luck! More common, however, is the mammalian model. We birth a new community and desire to nurture it along toward maturity and adulthood. The question is, how do we do that in a way that does not suffocate the planter? How do we empower the planter to thrive and succeed? The answer is found in identifying those areas where we can guide and direct.

FIVE WAYS A PARENT CAN GUIDE WITHOUT SUFFOCATING

Wise parenting is not about controlling, but rather, guiding. The following areas are where the parent church should exert guiding influence on the plant.

Planter Selection

This is a big decision that should take the most energy and time. The number one reason new babies fail to thrive is because the wrong leader was selected! Character and call are important considerations in discernment. Also important is the competence or giftedness of the planter. Specialized assessment methods are available to discern whether a candidate is "wired" for planting. Finally it is important to discern the "rightness of fit". Here you need a sense of confirmation that your candidate will have "chemistry" or "relational comfort" with the target audience you propose to reach.

Ministry Boundaries

A case can be made for several different church models in any given area. The parent should research what opportunities exist in the area. Different planters are likely to look at that opportunity through different lenses based on their background and experience. The parent can first set the parameters for the planter to explore. Those parameters are likely to be set by the core group from the parent congregation or the dominant demographic in the target area. Other boundaries set by the parent include the theological, ethical, and professional expectations that are in keeping with the call to ministry.

Regular Coaching

Every church planter needs a coach to help him work his plan, and the parent should use its influence to ensure a good one. The lead pastor of the parent congregation should not take this role because it can create a conflict of interest. The coach needs to be separate from the parent to encourage planter honesty, transparency, and independence. The parent can, however, provide a stipend for the coach as a way of encouraging a deliberate coaching plan.

Clear Outcome Expectations

The planter needs to know early on what the parent church's expectations are for the plant. Those expectations could include the date of the first public worship, how long until financial independence is attained, frequency of board meetings and denominational loyalty.

Participation on the Oversight Board

Every planter needs oversight and accountability. The purpose of the Oversight Board is to provide a place where regular communication, accountability and support take place. This is the venue where the parent can be best informed and speak into the process. The Oversight Board exists until the new church is self-governing.

OVERSIGHT THAT EMPOWERS

It seems every church leader has a moment when he wonders how he got swallowed up by a minor issue that has become a major drain. Unproductive meetings and unnecessary bureaucracy will certainly kill a new church start. There are a multitude of logistics and leadership tasks associated with planting. Yet a pastor must also be free to build redemptive relationships with people in the community. Finally, the pastor must be accountable for the outcomes and progress agreed upon from the beginning.

John Kaiser and others have given clarity and definition to accountable leadership in ministry (*Winning on Purpose*, John Kaiser, Abingdon 2006). Their model, biblical and increasingly embraced by churches, identifies three team "plays" in congregational ministry.

The congregation plays ministry.
The congregation is responsible to use its spiritual gifts in ministry according to the vision of Ephesians 4. Each body of believers becomes the vehicle of ministry to each other and to the world.

The pastor plays leadership.
The pastor is responsible for oversight of the program team, alignment of resources and advancement of the vision. He is called to lead the body.

The board plays oversight.
The board is responsible for oversight of the pastor, the budget and the primary objectives of the church. They are the watchdog and authority for the church.

In this design for team ministry, the pastor (in our case, the church planter) is given great *responsibility* for results along with the *authority* to get the job done and *accountability* for progress in planting. If we fail to give the pastor any one of these three leadership prerogatives/expectations we are likely to set him up for frustration. Look a little closer at this leadership model.

ACCOUNTABLE LEADERSHIP

Planters need great authority and freedom, counterbalanced by clear responsibility and regular accountability, in order to achieve the quantity and quality objectives of the plant. The body where accountability takes place is the Oversight Team. The team should meet monthly from the very beginning and should be convened by the planter. Some planters will need to be coached to step up to this key role. Members should include a representative from the parent church, perhaps another area planter or a denominational leader, a financial person, and a mature core group leader. In coming months and years this team can morph into being entirely made up of qualified leaders from the new church. These are the trustees of the ministry and have a representative responsibility to guide the overall project. Failure to convene the team is likely to elicit a parental reaction down the line similar to the one described at the beginning of this chapter. The Oversight Team and planter need not communicate about the ministry programming details. These are the responsibility of the planter and his program team. However, the planter and team must review and track the goals, objectives, financial integrity and the overall planting plan. The Team defines the boundaries within which the planter can work the design and details of the plant. Issues calling for Oversight Team input would include hiring additional staff, setting the annual budget, change of location or ministry objectives and review of the planter's execution of the original plan.

Don is a church planter who is intent on building a trust relationship with his oversight board. He quickly selected and convened the Oversight Team (which included major stakeholders such as the parent church lead pastor, a denominational planting executive, a key core group leader and financially astute person). Each month he called the meeting and provided a report including his Ministry Action Plan (MAP) goals and objectives for the month. The financial picture, any deviation from the original design of the plant, and counsel being sought by the planter are included in this meeting as well. Only the annual performance review will exclude Don from his leadership of the Team. The parent has a place at the table each month to express concerns or support. This experience has yielded a growing trust between planter and parent.

Accountable Leadership Can:	Accountable Leadership Cannot:
• Attract better planters	• Promise a pastor job security
• Release planter for rapid progress	• Guarantee a successful plant
• Define and clarify roles for the team	• Keep everyone happy
• Correct unacceptable leadership	• Prevent unacceptable leadership
• Empower people to do their best work	• Guarantee the right leaders

GUIDING DOCUMENTS

Key documents such as a New Plant Plan, Articles of Incorporation and the Bylaws, can be effective tools for gaining clarity of the objectives and direction of the plant. These documents encourage trust and can go a long way in putting all parties at ease with the ultimate intentions and direction of the plant.

The New Plant Plan is the first document that should be created and therefore should be one of the first tasks of the planter. The New Plant Plan should include confirming evidence of the qualifications of the planter, information on the target community, how the planter will be equipped and coached, a 2-4 year overall projected budget (including outside funding sources and congregational giving), denominational affiliation of the plant, prayer support for the planter and the ministry, general time frames for public launch, and any other key ministry moves. The New Church Plan is a defining document that can call for signatures of key players.

Articles of Incorporation are important for setting up the non-profit organization, satisfying requirements for tax exemption, stating the purpose of the corporation, identifying the church with a denomination or movement, limiting liability, prescribing the distribution of assets and specifying how to amend the articles of incorporation. The Articles of Incorporation can be drafted at any point and should be agreed upon by the Oversight Team.

The Bylaws prescribe how the organization will operate. They should outline the organizational structure, prescribe the commitments to the denomination and provide broad theological perspective, describe the mission, define the leadership role and expectations of the senior pastor, board, staff and membership. It should outline those decisions that require congregational vote and any other legal provision to limit liability of the ministry. The Bylaws need to be agreed upon by the Oversight Team.

A Planter/Parent Covenant is a guiding document that makes explicit the expectations that parent and plant have together. A sample covenant is provided as Appendix B. A more detailed version of this, called an Expectations Interview, is often used in a denominational setting to make sure clarity is achieved for both the church plant and the sending agency. A sample is also provided as Appendix C.

Together the Plant Plan, Articles of Incorporation, Bylaws and Covenant help to document the intentions of the team. They are a way of confirming a trust relationship between key parties in planting.

IT'S ALL ABOUT TRUST

Few things are more important in any venture then the level of trust between its participants. In church planting, trust is critical between the Oversight Board and the planter. When trust is lost, there is a scramble for direction that threatens the potential of the new church to progress.

My discouraged planter friend retraced the tracks of lost trust as we sat together drinking coffee. He could look back and see his failure to convene his Oversight Board early, delaying them access to critical issues he was facing with the original intent of the plant. That delay precipitated a strong reaction from the parent church representative on the Board (along with the other members). The parent church also took responsibility for low trust. They acknowledged that their good intentions to design many of the details of the plant prior to the input of the actual church planter set the stage for conflict. If the planter had been involved in the process of discerning the target community and location of the plant, the outcome may have been very different.

Stephen Covey Jr. reminds us in his book, *The Speed of Trust* (Free Press 2006), that trust is built upon the credibility of the parties involved and a range of behaviors that ensure that trust stays high. Planters and parents come into a relationship with a measure of earned and granted trust. Over time, however, they both must develop trust. If a planter fails to do so, then the key stakeholders in the success of the plant will react by seeking control. If the parent fails to build trust, the planter will be tempted to reach his desired success by going around the parent. The following is a list of trust-building questions, based on Covey's insights, that can help discern next steps. This also serves as an excellent check-up for the Oversight Board and planter to work through together.

Do we talk straight to one another?
Is there enough time given for us to discern and express intentions and issues?

Do we show respect for one another?
Is there mutual appreciation for the challenges and perspectives we bring?

Have we clarified expectations?
Have we been precise and direct in expressing what we need from each other?

Do we listen to each other?
Are we paying attention to the deep concerns, fears and hopes we feel?

Are we practicing accountability?
Who are we responsible to, and is that relationship direct and open?

Are we demonstrating loyalty?
Have we been good stewards of the trust already given?

If either partner violates the relationship expectations such that trust cannot be rebuilt, a third party mediator may be required to bring correction or closure to the relationship.

TURN UP THE LOVE AND PRAYERS

Over the years I have had the privilege of assessing dozens of potential church planters. If at all possible, we seek to discern those who will be likely to succeed in this very difficult work. Much is riding on their leadership. We are careful to share with them that planting will try even the best prospects in unexpected ways, including spiritual adversity.

Parent churches can offer much prayer and encouragement to their planter and team. Perhaps the simplest act is to ask the planter how he and his family can best be supported and cared for. Ask. It is that easy. The insight you receive from asking can be used to encourage the ones who are on the front lines.

Questions to consider while navigating the landmine of Lack of Trust and Accountability:

- What is the "trust quotient" between your present board and staff?
- What "expectations for control" does your parent church have toward the new plant?
- How will your structure create a climate that encourages appropriate trust and accountability between the parent and the church plant?

Recommended Resources:
- *Winning on Purpose* by John Kaiser, Abingdon 2006
- *The Speed of Trust* by Stephen Covey, Free Press 2006

Chapter 4
Choosing the Wrong Model

"Even if you are on the right track, you will get run over if you just sit there."
— Will Rogers

merica's Next Top Model is a television show where would-be fashion models allow themselves to be shamed, starved, cajoled, and ridiculed in the hopes of eventually walking down the aisle fully employed. To some people, finding the right model is that important. Pick the wrong one and the product won't move.

Your church is in the process of reproducing itself. Imagine that you're one of the judges and you are looking at the church planting models on stage. The model you choose determines a lot. While there will always be nuances of how to do church (house churches, for example), the two most prominent models are Classic Church Planting and Multi-Site Church Planting.

Classic Church Planting

These days, "classic" is often associated with an old-fashioned way of doing things. For that reason, I don't like the term when it refers to church planting. In most cases this model is the preferred church planting choice. In classic church planting, a parent church recruits a church planter, whom they support in various ways. It's like parenting! The goal is for the new church to grow, mature, and become autonomous and self-governing. Eventually the proud parent will step back and let the new church become self-sufficient. There are many expressions of classic church planting, including:

Pioneering. A small team of leaders is sent out from the parent church with a specific target community or focus group in mind. This model requires a catalytic church planter with strong self-starter traits. The evangelism potential is high, and often efficient. Risks can be high, but such ventures are necessary and represent most of the church planting that happens worldwide. The parent church takes the initiative to see the church happen, but it more-or-less takes a hands-off approach once the team is out the door.

Branching. A significant core group is deployed from the parent church. This requires more faith for the parent church because things at home will certainly be different (leadership vacuums, income depletion, etc.) once the new church starts. It's always better for the lead church planter to choose who comes. The parent church grants a fishing license, but it doesn't decide who goes. Good parent churches take on a dignified, faith-filled approach, blessing those who leave and trusting God for future provision.

Colonizing. This method is similar to branching, but requires participants from the parent church to relocate. Normally this model is only achieved with medium-to-large parent churches whose resources allow them to address the logistics of helping families as they move, find work, and start anew. Again, the lead church planter determines who makes the team. I know of one colonization commissioning ceremony where the senior pastor of the sending church invited all of those who were moving to join their church planting pastor on the platform for prayer. To the church planter's surprise, many of the people who joined them on the platform had never been approved for the deployment. To no one's surprise, this resulted in significant values and agenda discord.

Partnering. Rearrange the letters, and "Parenting" quickly becomes "Partnering!" In human reproduction, we're prone to say that the healthiest offspring emanate from two-parent families. We can extrapolate and say the healthiest offspring also enjoy the benefits of being in a healthy extended family (with aunts, uncles, cousins, etc.). In Partnering, a parent church joins hands with other churches so that the risk (financial, spiritual, logistical) is reduced for everyone. Some parent churches can enhance their project by actively recruiting other churches to join the action.

Supporting. Churches can further reduce risk by inviting denominational expertise and resources to help the effort succeed. In conjunction with many of the sub-models listed here, many would-be parent churches benefit by seeking the strategic assistance of their association.

Unplanned Pregnancy. We know what this means. It means a new body is being formed in the parent without specific planning involved. Some people call this a church split ... or a potential church split. If this is recognized early enough, plans can be made for the birth to take place in a healthy way, rather than the usual rancor. Some churches simply need to recognize that they are pregnant and take proactive steps so that all parties land safely. Dan Maxton says, "When possible, wise church leaders seek to channel people's energy toward starting a new plant rather than dividing the parent church."

Legacy Planting. Some have called this "death with dignity." When an existing church chooses to close its doors because of population changes or declining success indicators, it can reinvest its assets into a new church that's equipped to reach the changing community. This can be a difficult choice, but it can also be one of the wisest stewardship decisions ever. Too often, a dying church will exhaust its assets trying to keep the organization afloat until the inevitable occurs. Why not make a bold decision and truly leave a legacy that perpetuates the body of Christ for the coming generation?

The Multi-Site Option

Multi-site church planting is when a parent church reproduces itself in other venues but maintains governance, missional endeavors, and financial control (one church, many locations). Some proponents of this model don't even like to call it church planting, but modern-day multi-site pioneer Jim Tomberlin (www. thirdquarterconsulting.com) disagrees. "The terms are really irrelevant to the community at large: It counts as a new church there."

Multi-site is trendy today, but surprisingly, it's not new. In fact, the first North American multi-site church that we know of is actually the oldest protestant organization in America. Dating from 1638 in New York City, a number of church planters collaborated for greater impact. The King of England granted these pastors a special privilege on Manhattan Island to form a single corporation under which four congregations were chartered. Known as Marble Collegiate Church (whose most famous pastor was Norman Vincent Peale from 1932 to 1984), this "collegiate" model for church organization has perpetuated for nearly 400 years.

Today much is being written about multi-site churches, and for that we can be grateful. The modern movement is quite young, so the data is incomplete, but churches considering muti-site need not proceed blindly. There are many solid resources available. Multi-site differs from classic church planting in that autonomy for the additional venues is not the initial goal. While the terms may vary, typically the original campus is pastored by the senior pastor who normally plays a supervisory role with the campus pastors at the other locations. In some cases the teaching (preaching) happens by a video venue (either recorded or simultaneously broadcast), so consistency of thought, mission, and vision is maintained.

Multi-Site Landmines to Avoid

Poor choice of a campus pastor. Those experienced in multi-site campuses agree that the biggest mistake a parent church can make is choosing the wrong campus pastor. Jim Tomberlin of Third Quarter Consulting (www.thirdquarterconsulting. com), says "the most important decision you'll make is in choosing a campus pastor. It's more important than decisions about funding, location, or delivering content. It will make or break a congregation. Pastors ask me, when choosing a person from the original team, do I choose an A leader or a B leader? I say, "Do you want an A campus or B campus?" Geoff Surratt, co-author of The Multi-Site Church Revolution, concurs. "The biggest mistake people make is to way underestimate the role of the campus site pastors. The key to campus site success? If you don't have the right leader in the right place, you won't have success." So, with this in mind, what should one look for in a campus pastor?

A track record of exceptional leadership, with the general traits of a church planter
• Above-average public communication skills
• A spiritual burden for a community or target group
• A person immersed in the DNA and vision of the originating campus
• A leader not given toward personal agenda
• A person who evidences maturity and healthy relationships
• A person with a track record of building and motivating teams
• Someone who has a genuine geographical fit with the target area

In classic church planting, we learned of the importance of assessing potential church planters ahead of time to see if they have what it takes to plant a church (See Chapter 5, Planter Selection Seduction). In multi-site church planting, assessment is equally vital. As multi-site plants become more common, we are seeing more assessment processes developed for campus pastors. Converge USA is one example of a church planting movement that is doing such assessments. Curt Gruber, co-director of Converge USA church planting, says, "there are numerous ways multi-sites are being structured. Some as satellites, some as pre-autonomous church plants, and others as a church-within-a-church. Some use video sermons only. Others use the multi-site pastor as a primary communicator. We're not assessing the model, per se, but rather the relationship between the two key leaders (campus and senior pastor)." Co-director Marlan Mincks adds,

> The second most important component in a campus pastor is the desire to work within a system that's already established. They must have a passion to own and implement another person's vision, but not with the plan to "learn and leave." In fact, that's really the big difference between that campus pastor type of candidate and a church planting candidate. Both must be catalytic leaders, entrepreneurial and outreach focused. What sets the campus pastor apart is that he needs to be able to internalize the vision of another and implement the mission for the sake of the ever-expanding call.

Expect to see more and more campus pastor assessment mechanisms emerge in the days to come. Make sure that your potential campus pastor attends a church planting assessment center or completes a thorough behavioral interview process before deciding to deploy. Look for an emphasis on being compatible with the senior pastor and existing structures. Insist on objective assessment; it will be some of the best money you can spend. It's one of those "pay me now or pay me later" propositions.

Finally, whenever possible, choose your campus pastor from within the original church/campus, rather than hiring from the outside—providing they fit the criteria for being a campus pastor. These candidates are more likely to reflect the parent church DNA and remain loyal. Those experienced in multi-site are nearly universal on this point. Charles Hill suggests that senior pastors choose team members they know because they've trained them and the candidates are already well respected by their peers and in their communities. "You risk betrayal, but it's a measured risk and it is better to choose people where there's mutual devotion to one another." Of course you should never use the multi-site venture as an opportunity to off-load disgruntled or under-performing staff. You'll still have to deal with them anyway, only now their impact will be multiplied. Bob Gustafson, campus pastor of Celebration Church, Green Bay, WI, points out that "if the campus pastor is chosen from within the originating church, make sure the candidate is adequately qualified and not just a convenient choice. If the pastor is likely to be chosen from outside the originating church, make sure the candidates have adequate time to take on the DNA of the first campus. This should be done prior to placing them into positional leadership."

Protectionism of the Parent Church. All churches should feel some intrinsic motivation to reproduce themselves, and all benefit from extrinsic motivation to spur them on "toward love and good deeds." In these days when church reproduction is a high value among church leaders, would-be parent churches need to evaluate their motives in choosing multi-site over classic church planting. While there are many solid reasons to go multi-site, the one sure motive to avoid is that of self-protection -- which asks the question "Is OUR church growing?" rather than "Is THE church growing?" If a church or its leaders are self-protectionist, multi-site can be tempting because the expanding flock is identified with the originating campus, and its pastor. As long as leaders are taking a sincere look at their motives (such as ego, fear, etc.), protectionism can be avoided and God can be glorified.

Underestimating Spiritual Dynamics. Related to the above, it's easy to start looking at church reproduction as trendy franchising rather than the spiritually-impassioned mission it truly is. Churches do well to enter into any type of reproduction with a sense of holy fear, understanding that they wage war, "not against flesh and blood, but against the rulers, against the authorities, against the powers of this dark world" (Ephesians 6:12). This is more than demographics and member-distribution maps. Seasons of prayer, fasting, and spiritual discernment are warranted. Prayer walks ("praying on-site with insight") and pleas for God's guidance will show a proper sense of spiritual dependency. Assess the potential campus pastor with spiritual passion in mind. Charles Hill says, "don't make the mistake of assuming that the campus site leader is spiritually minded. Assess!" Remember that any work of God is an open opportunity for dissension and seeds of discontent. Competition and pride can pit campus against campus. Prayer, humility, public affirmation of the leaders, direction of the church and spiritual dependency of every kind can position the mission for maximum health.

Cookie-Cutting. It's good to cast vision, but beware of casting that vision in concrete. There are dozens of iterations of the multi-site church. Each location will share certain similarities, but they will also have a uniqueness all their own. Sometimes this dissimilarity can cause consternation among stakeholders. Children never turn out exactly the way their parents envision. In fact, without care, many dysfunctions will reproduce themselves. Governance, staff relationships, and quality control will certainly vary, and there will be changes over time. Continue reinforcing this commitment to flexibility. Geoff Surratt says, "we've found that the closer the site is, the easier it is to manage quality control. But one of our sites is five hours away, which practically means 'no control'. One extra site is not that difficult. But no matter how many you start, know that it will be more difficult than you thought." Churches that adopt a multi-site model need to communicate that this is a faith venture, that this is God's work, and that things will change. I once heard Rick Warren formulate this commitment to flexibility as: "we'll never start a ministry that we can't shut down. We'll never put up a building that we can't tear down. The only thing that's sacred around here is God and His Word!"

Sticker Shock. I read somewhere that one of the rules for vacationing was to take half as much luggage and twice as much money as you think you're going to need! I guess that goes for church reproduction too. Multi-site can be cost-effective, but it's not without cost. It is a good thing to be sacrificial and faith-filled, but it is not a good thing to be presumptuous and haphazard. The words of Jesus give food for thought. "Suppose one of you wants to build a tower. Will he not first sit down and estimate the cost to see if he has enough money to complete it?" Luke 14:28. Consider these four categories of cost:

Direct financial costs. This would include rent, staffing, equipment, advertising, and so on. As with classic church planting, it can be projected that as the venue grows so will the income associated with that venue. The financial base of any church grows with "more pockets and deeper pockets." But as with classic church planting, it will take some time before newcomers ("more pockets") start helping pay the bills. In the initial stages of the new venue all that has happened is that overhead costs have increased. So plan accordingly.

Indirect financial costs. When our first son was a toddler he managed to ruin a television by pulling it off its stand. I don't know how that happened (bad parenting?), but he did it. I said to my wife, "Part of the cost of raising children is just replacing the stuff that they destroy!" There are always indirect costs for reproduction. Often when churches venture into multi-site plants, they ask their staffs to multi-task by investing a portion of their time on the new venture—either on-site or remotely. This can be an effective way to get the venture off the ground and maintain quality control. In the movement I'm part of (Converge Worldwide) we like to ask our pastors to "tithe their time to mission." Staffs can be stretched, but we need to remember that this has a price too. This might be termed "in kind" contributions. In addition to the hours devoted to the new site, there will be additional meetings and new procedures adopted to manage the venture. It's not hard for staffers to neglect their required duties at the original campus in favor of the pressing needs and immediate thrill of working on something new. So this should be monitored.

Emotional costs. Emotion can take a hit when reproduction occurs. In the human life-cycle, mothers often experience a postpartum depression.

Some of the thrill is gone and some of the reality sets in. When new churches or multi-sites are launched, there are emotional realities that can eventuate within the parent church or original congregation. For instance, some friends and acquaintances will relocate to the new venue. Some popular staff people may relocate as well. The original campus can then feel a sense of letdown because the church feels smaller. The corporate ego of the campus can suffer. With so much attention being given to the offspring, things can start to feel competitive. It's good to recognize that emotional dissonance can occur, and it's helpful to prepare for it and to coach the church accordingly. Lathan Duncan of Celebration Church in Green Bay says, "competition does occur over resources, but good leaders will communicate vision in many ways. Mention the advantages of being multi-site, with the benefits of large church resources and the intimacy of a small church."

So it comes down to casting a faith-filled vision. A friend of mine told me about a time when his church was taking a special offering for a specific project. People gave sacrificially, and unusually. In the collection basket a wedding ring appeared. What was the context of that? A divorce? The loss of a spouse to death? An inheritance? No one knows, but he told that story to the church, and insightfully declared, "We don't know what happened here, but we do know that someone was willing to trade in a dream for the sake of a vision." Church leaders do well to cast a similar vision, knowing that their congregations may pay a price emotionally when they start a new site, but the payoff will be worth it.

Logistical costs. These are related to emotional costs, expect that there is more stress because there is more to do. Geoff Surratt says, "Trying to be identical is stressful. In video venues, for instance, you need to time the production down to the second so things synchronize at the other sites. That's constant stress! And no matter how many sites you start, know that they will be more difficult than you thought."

Inadequate Communication. One of my favorite comedic lines comes from Steven Wright, who was describing a time he was going through United States Customs and Immigration coming home from Canada. Wright says, "I made a mistake crossing the border. They asked me if I had any firearms. I said, 'What do you need?'" Good communication requires an understanding of what needs to be communicated, as well as when and how to do it. For multi-site church plants, this will include communication:

- With the congregation, as you gain momentum for the project.

- Between campuses. Charles Hill warns, "don't assume that having the same logo and the same printed materials will necessarily coalesce the campuses!" The key to good communication is to have the senior pastor in meaningful relationship with the other campus pastors. It is hard to recommend a multi-site plant if a senior pastor cannot deliver on this. "The senior pastor must give time and input with campus pastors weekly – not just ministry related mentoring, but hanging out; constantly defining DNA and growing together," says Lathan Duncan. Jim Tomberlin echoes, "Campus pastors can give lip service to mission but really have their own agenda and vision. To avoid this, the campus pastors must be mentored by the senior pastor, not as a supervisor, but as a mentor. They are reflecting the original pastor, and you've got to be in relationship with them."

The wave of multi-site parenting is exciting, but unlike classic church planting we are only in the earliest days of learning the landmines. For instance, we don't know a lot about how multi-site churches thrive following the resignation or dismissal of the senior pastor. Avail yourselves of the excellent books, consultants, and on-line resources that are produced these days, and talk with those who are doing it.

Questions to consider while navigating the landmine of choosing the wrong model:
- What are the long-term implications for your church in choosing a classic or multi-site church planting model?
- If choosing a classic model, which of the seven sub-models works best for you?
- Is there a hybrid?
- Who can you partner with?

Recommended Resources:
- *The Multi-Site Church Revolution*, Geoff Surratt, Greg Ligon, and Warren Bird, Zondervan, Grand Rapids, MI, 2006.

- *A Multi-Site Church Roadtrip*, Geoff Surratt, Greg Ligon, and Warren Bird, Zondervan, Grand Rapids, MI, 2009.
  www.multisitechurchrevolution.com

- Third Quarter Consulting, www.thirdquarterconsulting.com
  Pastor Jim Tomberlin (pastor, speaker, assessment consultant)
  http://www.thirdquarterconsulting.com/

- Pastor Mac Lake
  www.maclakeonline.com/ and
  http://leadingmultisite.ning.com/forum/topics/resources-for-multisite

- Small Town Church Planting and Multi-sites
  Pastor Charles Hill
  www.thesticks.tv/

Samples of Multi Site Church Websites

- Life Church, Edmond OK
  www.lifechurch.tv/

- Seacoast Church, Charleston SC
  www.seacoast.org/

- Broadway United Methodist Church, Bowling Green KY
  www.broadwayunited.org/Joel/index.asp

- Bethlehem Baptist Church, Minneapolis MN
  www.hopeingod.org/MultiCampus.aspx
  www.desiringgod.org/ResourceLibrary/TopicIndex/64_MultiSite_Church_
  Ministry/

- Discovery Church, Blackwood NJ
  http://www.discoverychurchnj.com/multisite.htm

- Grace Place Church, Berthoud CO
  www.graceplace.org/default.aspx?pid=375

- New Horizon United Methodist Church, Champaign IL
  www.newhorizonchurch.org/html/multisite.htm

- St. Paul Lutheran Church, Ft. Worth TX
  worship.stpaulfw.com/page.php?page=template2.php&pageid=3ea4c7d77
  0b57ed3c25bd0490a6235a8

- South Mountain Community Church, Draper UT
  www.smccutahwest.org/FAQwest.htm

Chapter 5

Planter Selection Seduction

Be what you is and not what you ain't cause if you ain't what you is then you is what you ain't.
— Folk Wisdom

How do you not like some people? Take Fred for example. Even in his first call he demonstrated passion for ministry and an ability to preach. The church grew by 30 percent in the five years he served there. He had graduated at the top of his seminary class and had the pedigree that predicted success (both his father and brother in ministry). With that subtle swagger that pastors are allowed, he exuded confidence and vigor you could only hope for in a church planter. Young, with an attractive family, Fred surely would be a magnet to other young families. So when the plum opportunity emerged in a new denominational church planting thrust, eyes naturally turned in Fred's direction as a potential church planter. It was the beginning of what became a kind of "fatal attraction."

It's not that there was no evaluation process. Several leaders met privately to vet the candidate. They reviewed transcripts, references, and sermons. During interviews, the discussion was about how open the young family was to relocating several states away. There were conversations with the pre-existing core team and follow-up evaluations regarding chemistry, vision and values. When Fred accepted the financial package, which included an expectation that the church would be self-sustaining in four years, all systems were "go". So his family packed up and set out for their new ministry of church planting. Little did they realize they were about to be sifted in deeply painful and defining ways. Four years later they closed the effort in defeat.

It took years for Fred to make sense of the planting romance and train wreck. The feelings of hurt were mixed with a deep conviction of making sure that other church planting candidates had a realistic knowledge of the work and of themselves.

Planter and Assessment Motives

Church planting is a pioneer work that evokes idealistic notions for a lot of people. With the compelling case that planting makes for reaching lost people and capturing a new generation, many pastors, at some point in their journey, consider this call. The compelling stories that come from the front lines and the great need for planters heralded by denominational leaders also serve to entice potential planters. Church planting is often glorified and elevated in a way that can do a "guilt trip" on a pastor or young seminary student. To not plant would be to miss out on God's best. After all, even St. Paul vowed not to "build on another's foundation." In some traditions, church planting is even considered a "rite of passage." Before qualifying for any other ministry position, the expectation is that clergy have tried their hand and succeeded at planting a church.

There are intrinsic and extrinsic pressures that motivate some people to become church planters, and parent churches are wise to consider pressures when they begin the process of recruitment. If we expect to parent a new church successfully, it is critical that the motives behind leadership selection be clear. There are two foundational reasons.

First, church planting success rises or falls on the ability of the planter to lead. Selecting the leader is the most critical decision made in a church plant, and wise parent churches spare no effort in getting this decision right! Church planting requires a unique behavioral skill set that is evident by historical precedent in a candidate. Behavioral patterns are the best indicator of future success.

Second, colossal mistakes are made when people are pressured into church planting. When a new church fails, the ripples of pain go far and wide. We actually do prospective planters and their families a tremendous service in guiding them away from a position if they are not ready for it. This requires courage. A planter friend of mine once shared with some dreamy-eyed wannabes, "If you can do anything else with your life other than church planting, do it!"

Putting Your Plant in Neutral

Some time ago a pastor came to me announcing that his newly planted congregation was facing a unique opportunity to parent a new church. I quickly congratulated him and thanked him for being a leader among leaders! When I asked about what was unique about the opportunity, a big smile spread across his face and he declared that his son was feeling the call to plant a church just as his father had done! Then our eyes locked and I got the big smile too, as if to say, "this could be interesting!"

Fortunately, my pastor friend was very aware of the danger bias can have on leadership appointments. We all have our likes and dislikes in people that cloud our judgments when looking at the core qualities needed to lead. In the case of my pastor friend, how could he not be proud of a son choosing the same profession and challenge his father had! Of course he would commend his son to those who may consider joining his core team, donating money, or providing denominational oversight.

Bias is a powerful force that causes us to see some things that may not be and to be blind to things that others claim to see. We all demonstrate bias, and in church planting, bias can put very valuable things at risk. Thankfully my pastor friend knew that he was too close to the "unique opportunity" he had shared with me and he wisely requested a neutral group to discern the wisdom of his son being a church planter. That choice, which ultimately confirmed the young leader's gifts as a planter, resulted in significant trust and support surrounding the plant as things moved forward. That positive outcome only came about when those who were closest to the prospective leader relinquished their control of the outcomes and entrusted that decision to a more objective process. Frequently denominations will provide such services to their congregations. Other independent providers have emerged to provide a systematic, careful and reasonably objective evaluation of a candidate's prospects as a church planter. This can be expensive, but given the importance of the decision, it is money well spent.

Assessment Step #1: General Qualities

The following areas should be explored before proceeding with the expense of a formal, objective assessment of a potential church planter. Without these positive indicators, a candidate should not be considered for church planting at this time.

A sense of personal calling

Planting should never be a "fall back" career option. Sometimes good candidates have never truly considered planting a church until someone brings it to their attention. That's fine, but over time the candidate should clearly feel planting a church is God's calling for him. Nor should an individual "try out" planting as a second career option. Planting must be the candidate's first choice!

Spiritual maturity

Candidates should meet the qualifications of an elder in II Timothy and be recognized as such by a believing community. There is no substitute for good character in a ministry where spiritual attack is likely.

The planter's theological convictions should be in keeping with the expectations of the parent church. Church planting is not a good place to formulate core beliefs and values, though it can refine and deepen them.

Experience in ministry

Church planting can be a great career choice for a recent graduate of Bible school or seminary, but the candidate should at least have some experience in key ministry activities like preaching and leadership. Learning to plant and preach simultaneously is not usually a successful experience.

Financial stability

Often overlooked, the stress of debt and poor financial practices can overwhelm, distract, or add discouragement to the work of a planter.

Spousal support

In ministry, as in many other professions, if the spouse is not supportive and encouraging there will be a significant emotional price to pay. Spouses may not necessarily play the piano or rock babies in the nursery, but they must pray for and stand by their partner in ministry leadership.

These general areas of readiness can be discerned through interviewing, contacting references, and by directly observing the candidate. I often ask other church planters to spend time observing a prospective planter since they often have keen eyes for general qualities. Multiple sources of input only add to the confidence of the final decision.

Assessment Step #2: Behavioral Qualities

The contemporary work of church planting has been greatly helped by the research of Dr. Charles Ridley, who after studying hundreds of church planters, delineated predictable indicators of church planting success. After the importance of spousal support, he identified four additional key qualities.

Primary Behavioral Qualities

Visioning Capacity

A successful planter has a lifelong pattern of dreaming new ventures and projects that were successfully initiated, sold, developed, and established. These people enlist others into their dream. When necessary, they raise funds and work to overcome the obstacles in their way. They are creative in how they cast their vision and are energized by the things they start, whether a business, a club or a church!

Creating Ownership of Ministry

Planters have a track record of inspiring others to commit to and fulfill ministry positions. They actively pursue others who can handle tasks and then give away responsibility. They consistently see the potential in people and encourage them to serve for the sake of the ministry.

Intrinsic Motivation

Effective planters are internally motivated, thriving on accomplishing multiple tasks in a day. They enjoy a demanding schedule and use excellent time management skills. They also strive to excel and consistently give their very best.

Reaching the Unchurched

Positive prospects enjoy building relationships with unchurched people and leading them to Christ. They currently have multiple relationships at various places of commitment. They have a knack for starting spiritual conversations with people and can be found anywhere in the community – not just the church.

Failure to evidence a significant pre-existing behavioral track record in these four primary behavioral areas will result in a "not recommended" conclusion of the candidate by a careful assessment team. Secondary behavioral qualities also provide valuable insight to those responsible for the leadership decision. These areas are as follows:

Secondary Behavioral Qualities

Effectively Builds Relationships
Evidences the ability to meet new people and engage them in relationship.

Committed to Church Growth
Embraces growing the church numerically and spiritually. Candidates will leverage known principles of growing a church.

Responsiveness to Community
Understands local communities and implements culturally responsive ministries.

Uses the Giftedness of Others
Assesses, develops and releases others to serve where they are gifted.

Flexibility and Adaptability
Negotiates change successfully while staying centered on the overall vision.

Building Cohesive Groups
Orchestrates widely differing people to function as a unified body.

Resilience
Stays on course despite major setbacks, disappointments and opposition.

Exercises Faith
Evidences a strong relationship with God and willingly takes faith risks.[1]

The Behavioral Interview

The genius of Ridley's system is the recognition that the strongest predictor of future results is past behavior. Most assessment models today are based on his work, including a one-day "behavioral interview." These behavioral qualities are not specific to any particular church planting model or type. A person who can give very few examples of the above four "Primary Behavioral Qualities" would not be recommended to plant a church. Carefully designed questions, and carefully designed rating norms, result in a score that a skilled assessment team can provide to a parent church. The Ridley system has been formatted in a variety

---

[1] *The Church Planter's Assessment Guide* by Robert Logan and Charles R. Ridley, ChurchSmart Resources 2002

of provider programs, requiring trained assessors to administer successfully. A behavioral interview may take weeks or more to set up, but it is well worth it.

Assessment Centers

Another common form of assessment is known as the Assessment Center. Unlike a behavioral interview which analyzes one church planting candidate (or couple) at a time, the assessment center brings together a number of candidates at one time to determine church planting suitability. Each candidate usually is accompanied by at least one associate assessor from his denomination. Together with the resident assessment team, there are multiple observers and recorders of the candidates over several days.

Typical assessment center experiences will include observing the candidates' informal behavior (how they build new relationships and interact with the process) as well as their performance behavior through specific exercises (team building, strategic planning, preaching). Assessment centers typically include a battery of psychological tests and evaluations. The genius of this system is the concentrated presence of observation through multiple assessors over a compressed time that is designed to simulate the challenges a planter might face. Whichever model is chosen, church planter assessment is an essential step that must not be circumvented.

Assessment Step #3: Local Fit

While the discernment of these first two steps is best done with a neutral objective team of assessors, the final area of discernment can only be done with the help of those closest to the actual context of the plant. Their bias is welcomed and needed!

It is unlikely that a person raised in an urban setting will be successful planting a rural church, even if they passed each of the first two areas of assessment. Instincts, experience and comfort have significantly shaped each of us in ways that help us unconsciously "fit" where we live. Because church planting is an incarnational work, bringing the gospel to a particular people and a particular place, it requires a person who naturally fits into that setting.

A good way to discern a planter's local fit is to simply spend time with him in the environment of the plant, giving occasion for others to meet and experience him. Most people will quickly discern if the planter will easily fit into the target community of the plant. If the fit isn't there, it doesn't mean the person shouldn't plant a church, it just means that it should probably be somewhere else.

Candidate Abuse!

While these assessments are generally positive, the reader should be warned not to use them to abuse a candidate. Remember, these assessments determine suitability for church planting at this time. A significant number of planters will fail assessment protocols, yet carry within themselves a significant call and capacity to plant a church. Sometimes that call is squelched by an evaluation that glibly suggests that this candidate is not planter material. Good assessment allows a place for "conditional" approval. Church planting could be in the candidate's future if a particular issue or set of issues is addressed.

I will never forget John. He came to my office seeking confirmation to plant a church. We took him through a Ridley Behavioral Interview. When we concluded, it was clear that John had failed the interview. In a key area (Reaching the Unchurched) John had little past evidence upon which we could offer a passing score. It was a painful conclusion, however we were careful not to project a finality to his score. I challenged John to take at least a year to be coached by a person with an active evangelistic lifestyle. A year later John returned and he shared with me multiple stories of people he had led to Christ. There was a new excitement and joy in his life! We immediately revised his Behavioral Interview and today he is actively planting a successful ministry.

No one's life can be completely captured in one evaluation experience. We can change. Over time we can acquire a new set of skills, abilities and even passions in our lives. I'm not saying that anyone can lead a church plant, but rather, when God calls a planter, it may require a season of training and development. It is a grave mistake to deny a candidate's sense of calling on the basis of an assessment experience. Rather, we should come alongside that person and encourage him to grow and press into what God is calling him to be. In the case of a parent church disqualifying a potential candidate, keep in mind that you may be an important conduit in helping him find his eventual calling.

The lesson of this chapter is to be aware of bias when considering candidates to plant your daughter church. Don't assume a "keeper" too quickly. Don't assume rejection either. Dave is a planter who launched his first church at 61 years of age. He naturally attracts people younger than himself while remaining true to who he is. It is a delight to see his planting qualities flow from his leadership. God's call rests where it will when people respond to His calling in their life.

Don't assume qualifications or dismiss them. Always seek objectivity, for the sake of the church plant and for the sake of the candidate.

Questions to consider while navigating the landmine of Planter Selection Seduction:
- How will you ensure objectivity in planter selection?
- What biases are you likely to bring to the process of selection?
- What unique features of your target group do you need to consider in your planter selection?
- What amount of prayer have you invested in seeking a leader for your new church?

Recommended Resources:
- *The Church Planter's Assessment Guide* by Charles Ridley & Robert Logan, ChurchSmart 2002.

Chapter 6

Underestimating Environmental Risk

Throughout my years in church planting I've gone through several paradigm shifts relative to the reasons for success and failure in church planting. I once assumed that anyone who loved Jesus, and used our direct mail piece, could plant a church. That assumption was dashed on the rocks after seeing several failures. Eventually my denomination realized that it could objectively assess potential church planters to see if they "had what it took" to do the job. When we started objectively assessing potential church planters, we avoided a lot of pain. Our success rate jumped to 70 percent. That was good. We learned a lot. We were better stewards of our personnel and other resources.

Unfortunately I made another assumptive leap. I figured that as long as someone was recommended to plant a church by an assessment center or a behavioral interview, I could just ship them out to their church planting location and wait for them to report huge successes. Sometimes it worked out and there was a lot to celebrate. But there were other plants that languished, or even failed. My denomination asked why, which led to the next paradigm shift -- coaching! When we brought strategic encouragement to the equation by pairing an experienced church planter with a rookie, we saw our successes move to about 80 percent.

An 80 percent success rate is good—but it also means that 20 percent of those we were recommending for church planting were still failing. Real people with real dreams were being shattered. Church planting takes a human toll. We asked ourselves what was missing? What separated the 80 percent from the 20 percent?

I was traveling with my friend and colleague, Jeff MacLurg, to one of our regional church planting meetings one day when this issue came up. Why did our success rate not rise beyond 80 percent? We wanted to be good stewards and wondered where our stewardship was lacking? In addition to assessing (making sure we had the right people) and coaching (helping the planters make good decisions), there had to be another element that would raise success and reduce failure? Then it hit us -- environmental risk factors.

What are "risk factors"? In the medical world, risk factors such as family history or lifestyle choices (smoking, exercise habits, diet, etc.) can predict the onslaught of a disease or a significant health concern. For instance, a few people have died of colon cancer in my family. My doctor is aware of that risk factor in my life and takes a cautious approach in regard to it so I won't fall victim to the same disease that has brought premature death to others in my family.

When we refer to "environmental risk factors" in church planting, we're looking at safety issues that are unique to a particular situation or environment. My denomination has isolated eight risk factors that I'll share later in this chapter. But for now, please understand: it's possible to take a very qualified church planter (someone who's been objectively assessed), coach him well, and put him in a situation where the risks are entirely unmanageable—leading to failure.

Consider some of your church planters. Presumably they would assess out objectively as "recommended for church planting." They possibly received some strategic coaching. Things went really well for them. Now, take these same church planters and imagine putting them somewhere entirely out of their element. Reduce their resources. What if they had no like-minded friends working with them and were serving in a place where the culture is totally foreign? Is it possible that they would hit hard times and even fail? Of course it is. Show me a successful church planter, and I can create a situation where he would fail. If you were to drop me into downtown Baghdad, with no money, no friends, and no cultural connectedness, I would fail.

Jeff and I started comparing church planters to church planters and determined that given the constants of assessment and coaching, it was the environmental risk factors that were foretelling the degree of success and failure. We performed a rudimentary statistical analysis and came up with eight factors that created a predictive mosaic. Four of the factors carry more weight, so we refer to the groupings as "strong factors" and "moderate factors." The cumulative score will help us determine if this planter is a good risk for the target community.

THE FOUR STRONG FACTORS

We grade the strong factors on a scale of 1 to 5. (The moderate factors are graded on a scale of 1 to 3.)

1. How will you be personally funded?

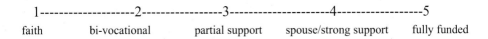

1	2	3	4	5
faith	bi-vocational	partial support	spouse/strong support	fully funded

By "Personal funding," we're talking about how a church planter's bills are paid. There are a variety of ways to fund this, but some ways have more risk than others. If the planter goes "by faith", it means that he is not sure how he'll pay his bills, but believes that something will work out and God will see him through. He could be bi-vocational, working another full time job while planting the church. He could have "partial support", meaning he has raised some money from outside sources, but is duct-taping his income together with a part-time job. Another scenario would be that the church planter relies solely on his spouse's income or has raised enough support to "get by." Finally, he could be fully funded by raising support, being on the staff of a parent church, or maybe he started by being independently wealthy. (Hey, it happens!)

2. Does the site selection match your cultural background or experience?

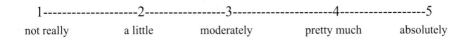

1	2	3	4	5
not really	a little	moderately	pretty much	absolutely

The question of cultural fit is somewhat subjective, but most of the time we can hazard a guess. Don't think of this question in terms of climate and geography (that comes later); rather, think of it in terms of the natural fit with the ebb and flow in the community. If the church planter has always lived in an urban environment, but is now thinking of church planting in a rural area, we'd give him one point. If the planter grew up in a small town, loved living in small towns, and is considering church planting in a small town with the same sort of cultural trappings as his history, he'd earn five points.

3. How many ministry partners will move with you?

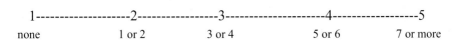

1	2	3	4	5
none	1 or 2	3 or 4	5 or 6	7 or more

Ministry partners are those volunteers or quasi-staff who are called by God to the project, just as the church planter was called. They are willing to pull up stakes, if necessary, and move with the church planter to the target community. These are people who have some history with the church planter. They have a common language and understanding of the vision. Value and agenda harmony issues are pretty much settled. With more ministry partners comes reduced risk. For example, if a youth pastor from a parent church becomes the church planting pastor for the daughter church, presumably he would have some meaningful relationships (ministry partners) to bring with him. But if the church planter drops in on a new community by himself, he'd tally just one point.

4. How many pre-existing adult contacts (individuals or couples) are likely to become part of your team?

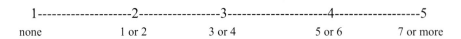

| none | 1 or 2 | 3 or 4 | 5 or 6 | 7 or more |

Pre-existing adult contacts are not the same as ministry partners who are already called to the new project. These are people who live in the target community. They may or may not be Christians. Perhaps they've expressed some interest in the new church. Maybe they're just a "friend of a friend" but can become a starting point for making contacts in the community. Obviously, there's some advantage when the church planter has a running start. If a parent church is looking to start a daughter church in an area where contacts already exist, that's a positive.

With the four strong factors, it's possible to earn up to five points each (twenty points total). The higher the point total, the lower the risk. While we want to lower risk when possible, we should re-iterate that there will always be some risk associated with church planting. It's entirely consistent with our faith to take risks for God. More about that later, but for now let's look at the four "moderate" factors. These can earn up to three points each for the church planter.

THE FOUR MODERATE FACTORS

5. How near is your family, your spouse's family or a natural support group?

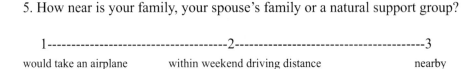

| would take an airplane | within weekend driving distance | nearby |

This becomes an issue when the going gets tough. Just like some of the freed Israelites longed to be back in Egypt, church planters will eventually hit some walls and long to be back where they belong. But if they're planting a church where they already belong—where they'd go back to if they had to—it gives them staying power and resolve. If things are going well, we don't long for our historical home as much. However, if we are struggling, we keep paging through photo albums, connecting with our old-time Facebook friends, and considering ways to get out of this situation and back to where we are comfortable. Related to this is the availability of people who can help with the intangible things, such as taking care of the kids while the church planters are away at a conference or retreat. It can be tough to be in a situation where, for a while, there's no natural support.

6. How closely does your ministry site approximate your geographic roots?

1----------------------------------2---------------------------------------3
not much   somewhat   quite a bit

Here's where geography fits in. Various sub-factors are hard-wired into the issue of geography, such as climate and recreational opportunities. Can someone from Texas plant a church in Wisconsin? Yes, of course. But they will be stretched a little, or maybe a lot. They may need to learn that church events should not conflict with Green Bay Packers games. (My friend, Pastor Terry Martell of Green Bay, tells me that the most important planning day of the year is the day the football schedule is released.) Can someone from the upper Midwest successfully plant a church in Hawaii? Sure. They'll like Hawaii for obvious reasons, but they may tire of it, too. Keep in mind that we're not simply talking about geographical preferences; we're talking about history and experience.

7. How close are you to other supportive churches who really want you to succeed?

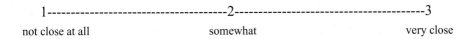

1----------------------------------2---------------------------------------3
not close at all   somewhat   very close

This is where being a good parent church really helps reduce risk for a church planting project. Alternatively, if a number of churches team together on a project, that is a tremendous help. In the human analogy, we tend to prefer two-parent families. If emerging churches are cared for by more than one responsible parent church, the payoff can be significant. We love what churches bring to the table: prayer, resources, encouragement. Parent churches are stacked full of resources, way beyond financial help. When one potential church planting couple I know visited what became their parent church, many church members said, "Don't worry. We'll take care of you." And they did.

8. How much vocational ministry success have you personally experienced?

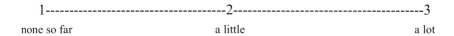

none so far	a little	a lot

Technically, this isn't environmentally related; it's experientially related. The question is whether the church planter is embarking on his first vocational ministry experience, or his first potentially successful ministry experience. Why does this matter? Experience brings know-how, and it brings perspective. Generally speaking, with some success under the belt, a church planter will have a greater degree of confidence and resolve when challenges come. My wife and I planted a church straight out of seminary; my first vocational ministry experience. It went fine, but I look back with some humor as I think about the times I was ready to throw in the towel—times which wouldn't bother me much now. Experience brings perspective and know-how.

With consideration of the eight environmental risk factors, we tally the results, and church planters are placed into one of three categories: high risk, moderate risk, and low risk.

8-15 HIGH RISK (Red Light): When a qualified church planter receives a score of "high risk," we recommend that they halt this plan at this time. There may be some pieces that fall into place and move them into a more acceptable risk category, such as raising more money or recruiting ministry partners. Or it may be an issue of finding a more suitable location. When someone scores in the high risk category, we're not saying they shouldn't plant a church; we're just saying that this plant isn't the right situation or the right time.

16-23 MODERATE RISK (Yellow Light): Moderate risk is acceptable, so we encourage the potential planter to move ahead. But it doesn't hurt to work on factors that could reduce risk. It's always better to be wise than presumptive. If God's calling seems clear, proceed with conviction and wisdom. If there is a strong uncertainty, then one should consider less risky opportunities or work to re-engineer the timeline. Remember: some risk is normal. The Great Commission does not call us to avoid challenging situations!

24-32 LOW RISK (Green Light): A low risk score is a green light. It seems as though God is in this so, with prayerful consideration, it looks like a positive situation. Of course there will still be challenges, but experience shows that this is a likely win.

The tool above can be helpful for parent churches because it can move them beyond presumption and toward wisdom. Remember, it's consistent with our faith to take risks. But it's poor stewardship to be presumptive. Parent churches can take a proactive role in helping reduce risk, perhaps by bringing more established churches into the project, committing more resources, or even altering the target location of the new church. Don't just dispose of potential church planters! Maybe there's a better fit for them somewhere else. Ask yourself: now that you have a risk score, how can you lower it? On more than one occasion I've held back a potential church planting couple until they could lower some of their risks -- and I've never regretted it. (For an unedited version of this Risk Factor Analysis, see Appendix D.)

Right now some readers are asking, "Isn't this just sociology? What about calling? Since when has expanding the Kingdom of God become a science?" I understand their concerns. Like anything else, we can swerve toward formula at the expense of listening to the Spirit. But here's my response: we are called to be stewards, and it is required of stewards that they be found faithful. This process gets us thinking clearly. Since adding Risk Factor Analysis to our protocol (along with assessment and coaching) our success rate has hovered around 90 percent. It's about being good stewards with the resources (personal and otherwise), so we make the most of what we have. Yes it is a formula, but it's one that makes us better stewards. Like Ahab seeking the elusive Moby Dick, I'd like to figure out that other ten percent. Church planting is more of an art than a science. And at the end of the day, it's a work of the Spirit. For now, I'm glad to close the gap on failure.

Finally, a word of caution. Keep in mind that this tool applies to potential church planters who have been recommended by an objective assessment process and who will receive adequate coaching. Don't just hand this Risk Factor Analysis to someone who is interested in vocational ministry. It may end up steering them down the wrong path. We want to be good stewards of all our resources, including those who may not be called to plant a church.

Questions to consider while navigating the landmine of Underestimating Environmental Risk:
- How might understanding environmental risk impact our recruiting strategy for church planters?
- What risks can we uniquely help to lower? How?

Recommended resources:
- *Risk Factor Analysis worksheet,* found as Appendix D

Chapter 7

Coaching Collisions

The heart of the discerning acquires knowledge; the ears of the wise seek it out.
— *Proverbs 18:15*

As a denominational leader, I was responsible for making financial grants to support new church planters. We were fortunate enough to have a fairly large fund from which to write support checks to planters who needed the boost during the early days of their work. Looking back, it's little wonder that people liked it when I came around! However, once my planters had received their funding commitment from my office, they did not seem real interested in engaging with me as their coach.

From the beginning of our vision (to plant 80 congregations in ten years within our region), we had placed high emphasis on every church planter having a coach. Coaching has been demonstrated over and over to be critical to success. Therefore I was recruiting and training coaches for planters. I was even trying to match coaches with planters. While these activities kept me busy, I was curious why few planters asked me to be their coach.

My "rich uncle" role came to an end a few years ago (we gave away most of our money), and with it came an interesting change in my coaching role. Suddenly, a number of planters began asking me to coach them. I accepted a manageable number and have gained new insights into the subtle, yet very significant, factors that make for successful coaching relationships. I've wondered about the change of interest in my role as a coach, but first some questions.

What is coaching? Why is it so important for a church planter?

The Fog of War

Most church planters go through an intensive planning phase in their work, sometimes called boot camp, during which they map out and design their new church strategy. During those days of intensive planning, the mission comes into focus and each phase takes shape in the mind of the leader. When boot camp is over and it's time to return to the field, anticipation is high and enthusiasm rules the day. However, this enthusiasm is usually short-lived and a few weeks into the plant, the planter has stepped on an unforeseen landmine. Unanticipated problems arise with details, logistics, money, or people. What once seemed so simple no longer is.

In military terms, the confusion that sets in during a major conflict is often referred to as the "fog of war". Confusion, bewilderment, disorientation and frustration are all part of this fog. Unfortunate things can take place in the fog, including friendly fire and lost ground. A communication link to someone outside of the war zone serves as a lifeline to the soldiers in that difficult situation. The same should be true for planting a new church.

When church planters step on landmines, where do they turn? We might be tempted to think that the parent church can serve in this role for fog-ridden church planters. However, for reasons we will explore later, that source is usually considered to be too close to be effective in guiding a new church planter.

Coaching is a link with a trusted source on the outside. It's a safe place for planters to disclose what they are struggling with, develop a plan, and work the process to move ahead. Without it, planters can bog down, lose perspective, waste time and miss opportunities.

Coaching 101

Coaching church planters bears little similarity to what you see on a football field or in a baseball dugout. The role of a coach in church planting is to help the planters work their plan. *Their* plan. For this reason, it takes a special person to be a coach. Sometimes great church planters are not very good coaches, and sometimes great coaches have never personally planted a church.

Good coaching is fundamentally about trust. The coach trusts the planter to have adequate insight into his context and a plan on how to advance the ministry. The coach also trusts that the Holy Spirit is at work in the process. The planter trusts that the coach can be a listening ear that will help him process the challenges that lie ahead, holding him accountable to make the right moves. If trust is violated, the relationship breaks down and the planter flies solo. Solo is not good.

Today, coaching is understood to be the "hands-on process of helping someone succeed." Many good books, seminars, web sites, and other resources are available to teach the fundamentals of coaching and to hone that skill. At its core, coaching involves a few carefully used skills:

Coaching Skill #1: listening. Listening is what everyone wants, including church planters. Their work is complicated with financial, methodological, relational, theological, familial, marital, and denominational stuff. When a coach gives time to listen to the planter, things begin to come into focus and mountains look a little less impossible. Good listening involves focusing attention, reflecting back what has been said, asking for more information, exploring the planter's ideas and clarifying assumptions. Good coaches do not need to say a lot to be effective. Though fundamental knowledge is helpful, they don't need to be experts in church planting.

Coaching Skill #2: ask penetrating questions. When coaches listen well, they have the means to ask very good questions. Not questions that push a personal agenda, but rather questions that clarify choices and direction. They identify values and priorities, increasing efficiency and fruitfulness. Good questions empower the planter to discover the solution to a problem and to own his role in that solution. This is not easy for people who are prone to offer advice and answers. Good coaches don't need to hear their own stories nor do they have to personally fix a problem the planter is wrestling with.

Coaching Skill #3: let silence do the heavy lifting. A good coach presses the planter with a quiet expectation that he be accountable for his progress. It's the planter who must determine his values and priorities and think through the ramifications of his choices. New coaches will often find these times of silence difficult. What purpose does this "dead air" between the coach and planter serve when the coach could easily fill the air with his wisdom? Nevertheless, we believe that the natural and spiritual processing that takes place in times of silence can be truly defining. The Holy Spirit speaks in moments when we make this kind of space.

A coaching relationship is driven by both the coach and the one being coached. The coach will be "a safe friend," who holds the planter accountable. In turn, church planters need to be coachable. The relationship is for their benefit and it is their responsibility to take initiative and be responsive to coaching. Most coaches will expect the planter to sign a covenant that holds him to the terms of the relationship. In some cases, a fee is requested. Paying for coaching services is generally a good thing as it creates a level of investment on the part of the one being coached. People generally invest their energy in those services that they have paid for! As a parent church, you can offer some suggestions of possible coaches, but leave room for negotiation, personal preference, and fit. If financial and personnel resources are invested, you may have the right to insist that the planter be coached. However, you should not prescribe the coach over the will of the planter.

Supervision, Advice, Coaching and Conflicts of Interest

Every new church planter needs supervision. He should be accountable to someone for the results of his efforts. This can include the Oversight Team, financial investors, denominational leaders, or the parent church leadership. Every new church planter also needs advice and wise counsel. This can come from a variety of sources including the denomination, the parent church pastor and other experienced planters. The problem comes when either of these efforts become associated with the coach. When that happens, we have a coaching collision.

Asking one person to wear two hats (a dual-role relationship), especially when it comes to coaching church planters, creates a conflict of interest that the planter realizes immediately – and will likely react to. My story at the start of this chapter illustrates a conflict that was played out in my role as a denominational funding source and supervisor. For a planter to engage me as his coach would require a high risk on his part. Rather than risk total disclosure, it is likely he would withhold important information from the coaching experience, especially if it might damage his potential to receive my funding provision. By withholding information, the value of coaching is immediately diminished. The planter cannot fully disclose his struggles or questions for fear of consequences. The dual-role relationship has contaminated the coaching environment.

This potential exists particularly where parent church pastors find themselves in the role of the coach. At first blush, they want to guide their new church according to the values and intentions of the mother church. However, things rarely turn out well when the parent church pastor is also the coach. The parent church pastor is better suited to serve in a supervisory role, leaving coaching to someone who wears no other hat. Your planter needs a supervisor to hold him accountable for the goals of the plant. Your planter also needs advisors to provide the best practical wisdom for his new ministry. He also needs a coach who is unencumbered by other agendas so that he can help the planter work his plan! The following are examples of dual-role relationships that can easily backfire.

Coach/Senior pastor:
In this scenario, the senior pastor might inject opinion into coaching, causing the planter to feel undue pressure to follow. The planter could be tempted to under-report struggles or frustrations out of a desire to please the parent church leadership.

Coach/Denominational leader
To some degree this pairing depends on denominational polity and the degree to which denominational officials "own" the church plant. Even when the new church has a voluntary association with the denomination, the denominational leader still exerts a level of positional authority over the plant. This can lead to a relationship marred by lack of honesty.

Coach/Key plant lay leader
When the coach is also a participant in a new church plant, a stilted relationship ensues. Here the planter is susceptible to several dynamics that confuse the coaching agenda, including differing interpretations of events, interpersonal conflicts involving common friends and congregants, and the likelihood of the coach having strong opinions about events that impact him personally.

Who makes a good coach?

It is unlikely that the person who coaches your planter will be exclusively a coach in his professional life. Good coaches can be teachers, church planters, area pastors, counselors or business leaders. The keys are for them to have had some training and experience in coaching as well as having the time to coach. Coaching requires 2 to 4 hours a month for meeting, record keeping and preparation.

Good coaches are people who build trusting and mutually respectful relationships. They are perceived as caring and have grown past the need to clone their own behavior in other people. They like to empower people, ask good questions, listen to and intuit where God is at work in a planter. They don't assume ownership or ultimate responsibility for the success of the church plant, rather, they turn that back upon the planter. They aren't afraid to challenge the planter to be better or do more. Coaches are empathetic and caring, but their first agenda isn't to be nice. Their goal is to help the planter achieve his primary agenda. Coaching brings resolve so that everyone wins in the end.

Steve Ogne and Tom Nebel offer the following list of coaching qualities:

Look for people who:
- Have good character
- Share similar core values and vision
- Are loyal to the planter
- Are respected by other leaders
- Empower others for ministry
- Have a teachable spirit
- Have the ability to lead and multiply a ministry
- Have the ability to listen and care
- Have the ability to strategize and train
- Have the ability to challenge and confront

Avoid people who:
- Have a problem with pride
- Need to lead rather than coach
- Need to control others
- Are over committed to other ministries

Finding a Coach and Engaging His or Her Services

After reading about the characteristics of a good coach, you may be wondering if this highly specialized person even exists! However, the church planting movement is spreading across North America and there is an increasing awareness of the importance of this role and training to support the effort.

A good way of connecting with potential coaches is to contact denominational leaders, local church planters or pastors. They often have a systematized way of helping parent churches connect with potential sources. Church planting boot camps are a good source for coaches. In that rich environment of learning and planning, coaching is highly valued and is a common point of conversation by planters who are looking for a good coach. It could take some time for all parties to settle on a good coaching fit. Don't expect to arrange a perfect match. Allow the planter to initiate the relationship and discern the compatibility. Give him time, but expect progress in finding and developing this key relationship. If possible, your planter and coach should both attend the boot camp together to jumpstart their working relationship. Monthly coaching appointments should receive financial compensation – including expenses. This will add cost to the planting effort, but money spent in developing the coaching dimension of a plant is rarely wasted. Coaching is too important to church planting to be ignored, minimized or overlooked. Parent churches must avoid this landmine!

Finally, remember that the primary relationship in coaching is between the planter and the coach. As a parent congregation, you can be helpful in finding and funding the coach, and you can expect coaching to be part of the planter's experience. However, after the coach selection is approved by the planting team, the coach can be virtually invisible to everyone but the planter. It is appropriate for those responsible for overseeing the plant to talk with the coach to confirm the relationship is active and vibrant.

Field Report

Over the last few years I have begun to hear the reports of those who have been on the receiving end of coaching. Mike, for example, is doing ministry in a community devastated by economic upheaval and job loss. It is a ministry context that developed after he arrived and it blindsided him. When we asked about his coaching experience, he flashed a big smile and reported how much that link meant to him. Things were tough, but he could count on his coach to help him process his thoughts and feelings. Together they talked next steps on strategy, discussing whether he would become bi-vocational and how his ministry could respond to what was happening in the community with so many leaving. Many voices were advisory to his thinking, but only one voice was committed to coach him forward.

Mike is staying on the job in his community despite unexpected challenges. Like so many other ministry leaders and planters, his coach has proven to be a key support for him.

Questions to consider while navigating the landmine of Coaching Collisions:

- Who will be responsible for the supervision of your church planter?
- How will you empower your planter to make good use of a coach?
- How will you budget for the services of a coach?

Recommended resources:
- www.coachnet.org
- *Coaching 101* by Robert Logan and Sherilyn Carlton, Church Smart 2003
- *Empowering Leaders through Coaching* Ogne and Nebel, Church Smart 1996
- *Start Coaching in Ten Minutes* by Tom Nebel, Appendix E

Chapter 8

Feast or
Famine Funding

*In life there are really only two tragedies. One is not getting what you want
and the other is getting it.*
— Oscar Wilde

I should have seen it coming when the point person from the parent congregation dropped a three-inch thick binder in front of me labeled "Church Plant Proposal". I gratefully accepted their research and appreciated being asked to review the details. So I went to work, but I sensed a landmine in the making.

The parent church was a large upper-middle class church that had a great heart for mission. Under the leadership of their pastor, a former church planter himself, they were now poised to release significant energy into planting churches. The immediate opportunity was a nearby ethnic community which was under-served by gospel-centered churches. At issue was the proposed amount of financial support. This plant would target the unchurched who had no understanding of stewardship. Furthermore, the socio-economic realities of the target community made it obvious that they couldn't offer much funding for the plant. Altogether, the parent was proposing to invest over $300,000 in funds to start up the new ministry. I listened carefully and then let the conversation go silent.

As a person with access to denominational funds, I was being put on the spot. The case for planting this church was crystal clear. The cost, however, put a lump in my throat. For us, this would be an unprecedented amount of money for one church plant. I returned to my office knowing that regardless of whether I chose to support or question the funding plan, I was going to have to provide solid reasons for my decision. Even if we could justify that much money, I wondered if it was it in the best interests of this new ministry to begin that way?

INSIGHTS FOR A FINANCIAL FEAST

At first glance, who can argue with a financial windfall? The planter has the good fortune to be able to dream and set his sights high. But what seems good at first glance may not be good in the long haul. Foreign missionaries have long recognized the downside of indigenous ministries receiving large amounts from foreign sources. A humble ministry receives a large gift from a generous donor, only to find that this supposed blessing backfires. The "law of unintended consequences" takes over. For example, local people give less. Those same local people who benefit from the ministry now feel a decreased level of ownership, sensing that someone else is ultimately responsible for sustaining it. Economic dependency begins to cripple what might have been a vibrant ministry. With local giving hamstrung, the ministry becomes vulnerable to the good graces, or bullish markets, of a distant benefactor. Sometimes the local ministry leader assumes a greater accountability to that faraway giver than to the local people he serves. When new financial challenges arise, people again look to the deep pockets of a faraway benefactor because their own resources have never been committed to the ministry vision. As the saying goes, money becomes like fertilizer. A little bit produces growth, but a lot only burns!

So what does this have to do with church planting? A well-intentioned parent can easily fall into the trap of being an enabler of economic dependency. Churches want to bless their new baby with plenty of resources, in some cases purchasing them property or providing for additional staffing. But by doing so, they can spoil the child. The planter happily receives those gifts, particularly if he is uncomfortable with raising the subject of money with new believers. Furthermore, an over-generous parent church can set a standard of giving that prices them out of the market of future planting opportunities.

Recently I had the privilege of working with an experienced planter in a situation where a large grant was provided for the project. It was such a sizable amount that the ministry could have taken an initial leap forward by adding full-time staff and purchasing property. Because of his considerable experience, the planter was given unusual discretion in how the money would be spent. But, despite the latitude he was granted, he decided to parcel the resources over several future new plants. He concluded that beyond his personal needs and modest start-up funds, the local ministry would be healthiest if funded with local dollars from new believers.

INSIGHTS FOR A FINANCIAL FAMINE

Most church planters and parent congregations will be far more familiar with the circumstances of financial scarcity than financial abundance. As I write this, our country is mired in its worst recession since WWII and people who have been investing in their retirement portfolios their whole lives are watching their value dissipate. It's precarious, especially for those non-profits who have built their livelihoods on large donations from a few plum givers. Economies will ebb and flow, clearly affecting our funding realities. There are warnings here for those who depend on a very few generous people for start-up funds.

The vast majority of charitable giving in North America (some say as high as 85 percent) comes from individuals, not from organizations. Furthermore, those who do the majority of giving to charities and non-profits are median income people. Ironically, a great many non-profit leaders violate the statistical trends and seek donations from organizations (churches) more than they do individuals. After being turned down by a few deacon committees, ministry leaders sometimes conclude that all the money is committed. Not so! A far more sensible approach is to return to the biblical command to grow individual stewards, regardless of economic class. The funding challenge in starting your daughter church, if shared among many average people, can potentially raise significant funds and provide financial stability. Development leaders remind us that congregations often raise 2 or 3 times their annual budget for building a new sanctuary or education space. Where does that money come from? The answer is the people's pockets. People have different mental categories for their resources. Their "tithe pocket" is not the same as their "vision pocket." The key is to make an appropriate appeal for people to consider a different pocket from which to give to your church plant. When you touch their hearts with a new vision for ministry you can expect a positive response.

Not many ministry leaders are hard-wired for fund-raising. We resist it for many reasons. But if we look at Scripture, we see a paradigm that should guide planters and parents who face this challenge.

Reality # 1   God owns it all.
There is never a shortage of money, only a shortage of stewards. This simple fact is a radical motivation.

Reality # 2   People are stewards.
The person asking me to consider giving is doing me a favor by offering an opportunity to steward what is not mine and that one day I will be held accountable for.

Reality # 3   Stewardship is learned.
No one naturally aligns their monetary values with the Kingdom of God. Stewardship is a learned behavior, catalyzed by an outside stimulus.

As leaders embrace this paradigm, fundraising becomes stewardship development. And stewardship development is not a means toward ministry, it is ministry! Helping people grow in the grace of giving will touch their lives as disciples. Where treasures begin to move, hearts start to follow! Stewardship development can grow the hearts of your congregation for parenting a new church!

PRINCIPLES IN BUILDING A FUNDING PLAN

The following key principles can help you reach your funding goals for your plant.

Think sustainability

Setting a budget for a new church is a significant issue. It depends on a lot of variables. A key issue is to pre-calibrate your plant for long-term fiscal sustainability. The big concern I had with the opening story of this chapter was that the well-meaning parent church was proposing a financial package that was out of step with the eventual financial sustainability of the new church. Given the socioeconomics of the target population, it was simply unfeasible that the new congregation would be able to afford to carry on this ministry at that level after the funding ran out. Most new starts should be financially self-sustaining within three years. If it takes longer than that, it is likely that the planter or the target group did not have the capacity to maintain the level of funding they received from outside their ministry. A rude awakening results in panic or depression, which can stunt the growth of the church.

Leverage the planter

The number one resource a parent church has in achieving its funding goal is their new church planter. (If married, we're referring to the church planting couple.)   People give to people-- and this is especially true for visionary ventures such as starting a new church.   The planters themselves have either a winsome effect on potential donors—or they don't. A planter's failure or success in fundraising is the first failure or success of the plant. For a positive experience, it is often necessary for the planter to be coached and trained in the biblical and practical work of stewardship development. There are a variety of resources to help with this, and most "boot camp" experiences will offer such training. The parent church should direct the planter to take advantage of that training.

Provide contacts

In many cases the parent congregation will have budgeted money for the new start. However, this is not the giving limit of your church! I recommend approaching individuals too! Donors want to hear from the point person of the ministry they are being challenged to support. In many cases the planter has a shortage of potential or "qualified" givers. That is where a parent congregation can be enormously helpful. The rich networks of small groups and friendships are a fundraiser's dream come true! If the senior pastor holds up the need and creates large and intimate environments for the planter to tell his story and make an appeal, you will be surprised at how fast wallets open. If you are part of a denomination or affiliation of churches, the parent church pastor can introduce the planter to those leaders for networking. This process shouldn't impact your church budget because your people will be giving over and above their usual tithe (usually only about 3% of their income).

Other churches can help too, especially if they are part of a network of "aunt and uncle" churches that work together to see planting happen. Be grateful for churches that participate through unified budgets, but don't stop there! Do what you can to encourage those churches to expose their members, as individual donors, to support the work. If five churches contribute $100 each per month, that's great. But it is even better to have five churches that give us access to twenty members with giving potential!

Make the case

Every donor appeal requires a "case statement" that will speak to the heads and hearts of potential givers. The case statement is critical. While the parent church leaders are convinced of the importance of starting a new church, many average members are not. A good case statement is the product of the parent and the planter.

COMMUNICATING THE CASE

A case statement is the ultimate answer to the what and why questions people will have about the new work. Once completed, the case statement should be tested and refined so that the ultimate communication has persuasive integrity. The statement can be conveyed in numerous ways: PowerPoint, flip-chart booklets, flyers, websites, DVDs, YouTube, and many other creative ways. Meaningful photographs have touched the hearts of many potential donors. To touch the head of the donor, be sure to include the following:

What is our vision?

A great lead-off statement clearly and concisely communicates the vision. Vision is what you specifically intend to do as an expression of the work of Christ. An example could be: "God has called us to plant a new church in urban Kalamazoo to reach people who are living in the Stewart Neighborhood and have not yet responded to Jesus Christ. Our vision is to see a self-sustaining church in three years.".

Why is this church plant necessary?

Demographic or community survey work is included to answer the question, "Why plant a new church here?" Also, include the defining qualities of the plant that distinguish it as being well-suited to the environment proposed.

What is our track record?

Donors have the right to ask whether their stewardship decision is wise. This is your opportunity to communicate the track record of your congregation (if you have successfully planted in the past), and the planter. Some planters will have a worthy track record. In other cases, a confident statement of presumed success can be made because of the predictive nature of assessment, coaching, and risk factor analysis. If your denomination or fellowship group has success in church planting, highlight this as well.

What is the opportunity?

The idea is to communicate a special window of opportunity that is open now, with a sense of immediacy to act while the window is open. Maybe the need for a new church is urgent, due to a unique set of circumstances. Perhaps a prayer movement has created a groundswell of spiritual awakening. It could be that the planter has deep roots in the community or maybe the parent congregation is convicted of their need to "be fruitful and multiply"!

What is the plan?

State simply what your ministry plan is. What kind of church will this be and what general timeline is envisioned? The plan will help donors get a picture of what to expect a year into the project. Have a more detailed plan available for those who ask.

What is the cost?

Based on your detailed budget planning and projection, this portion should quantify the entire amount of outside funding needed for the start-up. Factor in anticipated giving by the new church attendees, and come up with a figure that reflects the total amount of funds needed from outsiders for the maximum three-years it will take to put the plant on sustainable ground. On one occasion a planter told me how he reached this moment and apologetically shared only a small portion of the need with a donor. The donor immediately wrote a check for the entire amount, leaving the planter to wonder if he had asked for too little!

Does this touch your heart?

Finally, realize that most donors will not give significantly if their heart is not moved. The person making the request needs to sense the donor's perspective. Whenever possible, meet with the donor only when his or her spouse is present. If this is their first exposure to the opportunity, they may need some time before deciding. Be sure to give clear instructions of how to proceed in terms of the mechanics (where to send a check, if they can give monthly, and so on). Wise fundraisers never use the phrase "one-time gift," which could preclude them from ever approaching the donor again. Use the term "special gift," to keep doors open for the future.

Raising start-up funds requires a lot from the planter, since it falls on him to passionately share his vision. It also requires a hospitable and supportive parent church. The leadership of the parent church can create an environment where a planter, and his team, can effectively raise the resources needed to reach funding goals.

ELEMENTS IN BUILDING A BUDGET

If possible, involve the planter when building the preliminary budget and the final budget for the new church plant. The budget might include the following elements:

Planter salary, benefits and travel budget

Remember that planters have unique leadership gifts that are worthy of significant compensation. By compensating them well, you are setting a standard for the coming years of the church.

Compensation for part-time staff
Staff positions such as worship leader, administrator or children's ministry leader may be appropriate to consider. Remember you are setting precedent here.

Rental space
Most settings require office and worship space that are congruent with the target audience. Don't forget liability insurance and utilities.

Advertising and communication costs
Be sure to include web design costs.

Boot camp costs
Other planter training and ongoing education costs should fall into this category.

Equipment costs
Items such as sound, seating and staging should be accounted for.

Programming expenses
What kind of nursery and children's ministry are needed?

Denominational or affiliation dues
What does your missions budget look like? If congregants see the church tithing from its budget, they may be encouraged to tithe as well.

The budget of a new start should be projected for up to three years. A plant will normally have a portion of its first year with no public worship (up to 6 months). This period will impact both income (offerings) and expenses. As time goes by, outside funding is scaled back proportionately. Remember to have your agreements in writing, and review them at appropriate intervals with the leadership of the new church plant.

FINANCE FIRST AND FINAL THOUGHTS

Stephen Gray outlines several key principles for funding a new start. It is wise to check out his careful reasoning in this area, but a summary here would be as follows:

1. Adequate funding is a delicate balance between funding too much and funding too little.

2. The planter should be leveraged in external fund raising but not to the extent he is overly worried about surviving or cannot do his work.
3. Fast growing plants do not receive outside funding beyond two years. They receive at least $50,000 in start up ministry funds.

Many churches forego participating in the joy and energy of birthing a new church because they believe they cannot afford it. Their first and final thoughts are a fearful "We cannot afford it." The reality is that, in church planting, money follows vision! God is speaking to people in your ministry and others around you about being good stewards of their resources. Your plant will come at a time that gives your people an opportunity to give. Jesus did not say the gates of Wall Street will prevail against his Kingdom. Funding is important. As with most important elements of successful church planting, it's also a potential landmine. Our work is to be obedient to the vision we receive and to trust that where God leads, He also provides.

Questions to consider while navigating the landmine of under and over funding:
- Is there a plan in place to adequately fund your new church plant?
- From the beginning, how are you preparing your plant for self-sustainability?
- What expectations do you have of your church planter for the raising of start-up funds?

Recommended resources:
- *Making the Case*, Jerold Panas, Institutions Press, 2003
- *Raising More Than Money*, Doug Carter, Thomas Nelson, 2007
- *The 33 Laws of Stewardship* Dave Sutherland and Kirk Nowery, Spire Resources, 2003
- *People Raising: A Practical Guide to Raising Support* by William Dillon, Moody Press, 1997
- *Planting Fast Growing Churches*, Stephen Gray, ChurchSmart Resources, 2007

Chapter 9

Launching Misfires

Self interest is the only immutable quality in the heart of mankind.
— Alexis De Toqueville

L eith Anderson is senior pastor of Wooddale Church in Minneapolis, MN, and an active proponent of church planting. He travels the country and teaches pastors and denominational leaders on the subject of planting with great wisdom and insight. He is also quick to admit that his insights have come through some trying experiences.

When Wooddale birthed its first church, significant anxiety arose over who would leave the mother church and go with the new plant. As the church elders began to look through the church roster and identify prospects, the first likely candidates elicited an enthusiastic "ah ha!" moment—quickly followed by some pushback. Comments were uttered such as: "Great people, but aren't they indispensable to Wooddale? We could be hurt if we released them!" So the board moved on to the next prospect, and again, brief optimism was followed by the cautious voice of reason. One person was a key giver, another was a key leader, and yet another was an indispensable prayer warrior. After a while the elders caught themselves in their lack of faith. After some soul-searching, they reversed their approach and released anyone in the congregation to join the new ministry. Today, Leith tells the story with a smile on his face. There's always anxiety attending a first birth! Most pastors and elders will feel the temptation of self-interest when they lead their church to reproduce itself.

John Maxwell reminds us of a biblical principle when he states, "Someone has to give up if anything is ever going to go up." Parenting a new church is a great exercise in "giving up," but as any good parent knows, giving calls for wisdom and good judgment. I have always been taken by Paul's prayer in Philippians 1:9-10 "….that your love may abound more and more in knowledge and depth of insight so that you may be able to discern what is best....". When it comes to giving, the good can be enemy of the best! Take a look at the different ways the launch of a new start can misfire.

Generosity Misfire

I recently read that it costs about $220,000 to raise a child through high school. For most of us, ignorance is bliss when it comes to financing our family dreams! Parenting a new church is costly too, but not always in the ways we imagined them to be. Most leaders immediately think about contributing funds or sending people. While that kind of generosity is helpful, there are more critical gifts to give your new baby!

Just as no two children are exactly alike, no two parent church experiences are exactly alike. I like to award gold, silver, or bronze medals to parent churches for their degree of participation in starting a daughter church. If a church starts a new church, it deserves a medal! All parent churches sacrifice, and some are positioned to "go for the gold"!

Gold Medal Parenting
To earn a gold medal, parent churches do the following:
- Surround the planter with personal support and friendship.
- Engage in spiritual warfare by praying diligently for the daughter church.
- Become advocates for the planter, helping legitimize the new work to a broader constituency of churches.
- Offer administrative help, office assistance, and other practical support during the pre-launch phase of the new church.
- Have a place on the Oversight Team for the daughter church.
- Provide financial support to help the plant in the early months and years of development. Also will help the planter raise funds.
- Release and recruit people to actively join the plant for long-term involvement as core group members.

Silver Medal Parenting
To earn a silver medal, a parent church will do the following:
- Surround the planter with personal support and friendship.
- Engage in spiritual warfare by praying diligently for the daughter church.
- Become advocates for the planter, helping legitimize the new work to a broader constituency of churches
- Offer administrative help, office assistance, and other practical support during the pre-launch phase of the new church.

- Have a place on the Oversight Team for the daughter church.
- Provide financial support to help the plant in the early months or years of the ministry. Also will help the planter raise funds.

Bronze Medal Parenting
To earn a bronze medal, a parent church will do the following:
- Surround the planter with support and friendship.
- Engage in spiritual warfare by praying diligently for the daughter church.
- Become advocates for the planter, helping legitimize the new work to a broader constituency of churches
- Offer administrative help, office assistance, and other practical support during the pre-launch phase of the new church.
- Have a place on the Oversight Team for the daughter church.

The point of this "medal ceremony" is to remind us that the core activity of a parent does not always involve giving a lot of money or throngs of people.

I am currently watching with delight as this principle is lived out in my part of the country. I know one bivocational planter with a remarkable evangelism gift. This planter received a denominational grant and was committed to doing a "parachute" plant (no core group of people). What was lacking was a parent congregation to provide prayer, emotional support and advocacy that was so needed in the area. At a local pastor's gathering, the opportunity was presented for a church to become a parent to this new venture. I watched as a pastor of a small church stepped up and led his congregation into the role of being a Bronze Medal Parent. In fact, the prayer movement alone unleashed by this church eventuated in dozens of new contacts and ministry opportunities for the planter. A year later the plant had a 50 person core group! Prayer is a powerful tool in pioneer Kingdom work! Observing the way they showered the church planter with prayer and support reminded me that every church can parent, and every parent church deserves a medal!

Regardless of the model or method whereby a parent gives birth to a new church, there is a sacrifice to be made. God holds us accountable to steward what we have, not what we don't:

[41]Jesus sat down opposite the place where the offerings were put and watched the crowd putting their money into the temple treasury. Many rich people threw in large amounts. [42]But a poor widow came and put in two very small copper coins, worth only a fraction of a penny. [43]Calling his disciples to him, Jesus said, "I tell you the truth, this poor widow has put more into the

treasury than all the others. [44]They all gave out of their wealth; but she, out of her poverty, put in everything—all she had to live on." Mark 12:41-44

Parenting is about pouring your resources into a new generation. And while that selfless work is not always noticed by people, it is noticed by God.

Blessed Subtractions Misfire

One of the landmines a parent church can step on is to take an entirely passive approach as to who will be released. As the saying goes, "You can fall off a horse on two sides!" When Leith Anderson and his elders recognized they were wrongly controlling who would go with the plant, they could have overreacted by sending anyone who wanted to go. But this course can leave the planter with a significant liability. Imagine the impact of a few "extra grace required individuals" on a new church that is birthed from a parent congregation of 300 people. One or two such individuals in a church of 300 may be manageable, but one or two of the same people in a launch team of 30 can present a significant distraction and liability to the planting pastor.

The leadership at Wooddale Church has developed a sophisticated approach to sending. First, they recognize that by "sending" they really mean a "calling." The Holy Spirit should be moving in people's lives, challenging them to partake in a new church start. After all, its not just the pastor that is taking a faith risk. Stories abound of people who have taken significant faith risks by participating in a new church start. Some double their giving. Others step up to serve in ways that stretch their comfort level. Still others relocate their work and families to be part of a new work of God in a given community. Leith Anderson recognized that he could present an opportunity, and challenge people to commit, but he could not pick who would go. Having said that, some people should be actively discouraged from participating. Planting is a spiritual battle and the planter should be focused on the people far from Christ in his community. Chronically needy or otherwise difficult people may need to be directed to stay behind. A church plant can implode if unhealthy people dominate things.

Eventually, Wooddale Church decided to invite some people to participate in a new church for a year – as temporary attendees. Some of these people would repeat this pattern several times as an expression of their calling. Others stack their worship, attending services at both the mother and daughter churches each Sunday. It's their expression of support. Some will go and never return. Leith notes that Wooddale attendees of less than two years are more likely to participate in the new venture. Such people have been involved in the parent church long enough to absorb the outward focus, but they've not been around so long as to become absorbed in relationships that they couldn't fathom leaving. Regardless of the method or model, the similar call, to be a person in the mission of Jesus Christ, is heralded clearly to the members of the mother church week in and week out. Some will hear the challenge one-on-one. Others respond to the challenge because of a sermon. All are released to the moving and call of the Holy Spirit.

Recruiting the Launch Team

The most common way for a parent church to assist church planters in building their launch team is to grant them a "fishing license." The planter is given permission to fish from the church, with the public blessing of the senior pastor.

The first step is to present the planter to the church. Advocacy occurs as the pastor and elders give visibility to and verbal endorsement of the planter's vision and leadership. This can take place through preaching, public forums, attractional events, or adult classes. Here the planter borrows the credibility of the key leaders as he or she seeks to establish his or her own direct legitimacy with people.

The second step is to give the planter wide access to the ministry of the church for sharing his vision with individuals and small groups. Here he can respond to questions and build relationships. Every dimension of the church should develop some relationship with the planter, including public worship, staff meetings, nursery, youth, adult, small groups, mission teams, etc. Several months of incubation build trust and relational capital for successfully recruiting. This will also give the launch team time to begin developing and maturing their vision.

Finally, people should have both formal and informal interviews with the planter before an invitation to join the plant is offered. "Interviewing" is not too strong a word for describing the work of the planter as he seeks a team that shares his values and vision. Not everyone the planter interviews will be welcomed on the team. We highly recommend reading the companion book, *Church Planting Landmines* by Tom Nebel and Gary Rohrmayer, paying particular attention to the chapter on Leadership Backlash. Agenda harmony is critical in the early stages of planting as tensions can take the planter's eye off the mission to reach new people. One very helpful mechanism for determining potential launch team members' compatibility with the church planter and his or her vision is called an "Expectations Interview". Each potential launch team member completes a survey, which provides discussion information for his interview with the church planter. It helps to expose preconceived assumptions as it brings dozens of issues to the table. For a sample of such a document, see Appendix C.

During this prenatal season beware of the launch team sealing itself off from outsiders. In fact, we prefer the term "launch team" to "core group" to avoid the implication that this group of people exists for itself. If the launch team meets for months in social and ministry environments, it can subtly become a closed community, ironically never becoming the outreach church it intended to be. The planter and parent are wise to guard against this phenomenon. Some parent churches have granted a "conditional fishing license," instructing the planter to limit his number of launch team members from the parent church to match the number recruited from outside the church. This gives incentive to build the launch team with an eye toward growth.

Low Birth Weight Misfire

During pregnancy it's not unusual for a woman to be asked if she wishes for a boy or a girl. The standard answer is, "I really don't care, as long as it's healthy!" That's a good answer for pregnant parent churches too. One factor that heavily influences new church health is birth weight, that is, the number of people committed to go with the new plant. Sometimes premature babies suffer with certain health conditions throughout life. The child survives, but there is a dramatic cost and stress in that experience that can affect that person for years. It's much better if the birth weight is normal.

Here's a good rule of thumb: one year after launching public services, a healthy new church is normally two to three times the size of the original launch team. In other words, a launch team of 40 people (a core minimum we strongly recommend) has a good chance of being 80 to 120 on its one year anniversary. Parent churches can influence a healthy birth weight by contributing a strong "prenatal" launch team size. This includes numbers, as well as a prayerful desire that the launch team be well-equipped with individuals who possess a wide range of spiritual gifts and other talents to contribute to the work. This is a serious work of the Spirit and participants should commit with intentionality. The desired birth weight of the church should be determined well in advance based on the overall design and financial sustainability plans of the plant. If the prenatal health is not strong enough to support that desired birth weight, it's wise to reconfigure the timeline and be health-driven, not calendar-driven.

As the team grows, periodically give them visibility in your weekend worship. Champion their effort as you lift them up in prayer and support. Your congregation is pregnant ... this is a reason for joy and celebration!

Pause Button

We've all heard the statement, "you never get a second chance to make a first impression." There is a moment of passage that is so defining that we can never repeat it. We get one chance! Oftentimes this is the case for new church starts. Yes, some can "re-launch" and take a second run at the mountain with success. However, more plants would benefit by pressing the "pause button" if they approach their public launch date and do not yet have sufficient people to form a critical mass. Under these circumstances it is important for the parent congregation to support the planter and encourage a delay in launch if needed. Ultimately it is the planter's decision. Launching is a high anxiety time for planters. They understand the importance of a positive launch and their need for quality people and critical mass to make that happen. Planters understand that after the launch they will be increasingly committed to programming weekend services and have less time for building new relationships in the community. If the decision is made to delay the launch, planters need the support of the parent as they work on evangelism efforts and building connections with outsiders.

My friend Jim was forced to delay his plant. He was encouraged that he had 65 adults in small group Bible studies, but that was below his goal for launch. Jim felt significant pressure. His parent congregation was waiting to celebrate that moment of "delivery." It was hard to wait. The people in his group were also eager to go public with weekend worship.

Despite the pressure, Jim adopted a simple formula that put the responsibility with the group. He gathered his parent and core people together and shared with them his desire to launch with a healthy birth weight as a new congregation. He described the circumstances needed to go public. When they had 75 people in small group Bible studies, they would begin to hold monthly preview services. Whenever those services were over 100 people for two consecutive months, they would begin regular weekly worship. With a sense of shared understanding they moved forward to a successful launch birth weight. As Jim looks back, he feels he navigated the critical birth process in a way that positioned the new ministry for bright days!

Questions to consider while navigating the landmine of casual launch team development:
- How do you plan to empower your church planter for recruiting new people to the plant?
- How prepared are you, though prayer and shared vision, to release those whom God is calling to join the new church start?

- How much time will you allow the planter to invest in the work of recruiting a launch team?

Recommended Resources:
- *Church Planting Landmines*, Tom Nebel and Gary Rohrmayer, ChurchSmart Resources
- *Values and Agenda Harmony Survey* sample, Appendix F.
- *Planting Fast Growing Churches*, Stephen Gray, ChurchSmart Resources

Chapter 10

After-birth Neglect

T he job of parenting is not over after a baby is born, in fact, it is just beginning! Churches should avoid the landmine of after-birth neglect, which manifests itself in three primary ways: Disconnected Involvement, Failure to Recover, and Intentional Infertility.

Disconnected Involvement

In their work *Churches Planting Churches*, Bob Logan and Steve Ogne popularized the human life cycle model of church planting. In many ways, parenting a church is like parenting a child, with predictable patterns of development for both the parents and the offspring. Simplified, there are four common phases, with attendant responsibilities of the parents:

Phase	Description	Parent Church Responsibility
Reproduction	The earliest phase, where leaders gain commitment to the vision and put a general plan in place.	Cast vision and encourage commitment among church members.
Conception	A commitment to a model and work to recruit a planter.	Empower the project through prayer, select church planter, approve the model and plan.
Prenatal	Essential ministry systems are developed and logistical issues are addressed, all with an eye toward a public launch.	Give sacrificially, bring guidance and encouragement to the core group/launch team.
Birth and Growth	Essential ministry systems are now implemented, monitored, and refined.	Be intentionally available to the new church, while releasing it to find its way. Work to recover and rebuild momentum at home.

The life cycle model is helpful for multi-site plants too, with the caveat being that a higher degree of control from the original campus is normal. In most cases, the objective is for the new campus to become mature, but not autonomous.

Avoiding Extremes

Following the general life cycle model, one obvious extreme to avoid is that of over-involvement. We all know what it is like to watch overbearing parents micro-manage their adolescent or even adult children. I remember observing a lakeside event at which a parent was barking orders to his child about wearing a life-preserver while canoeing—the child was over thirty years old! Some parents don't know when to step back, and the same can be true for churches, too. Children don't always turn out as parents hoped or imagined, just as church plants can be different than the parent hoped. It can be tempting to meddle, especially with issues related to style. Wise parent churches realize that stylistic differences are just that.

Alternatively, and on the opposite end of the spectrum, it's possible for a parent church to be under-involved. I joke with my friends that, unless there's a problem, I'm not really interested in new baby statistics. I guess it matters to someone that the baby is 19 ½ inches long and weighs 7 lbs, 6 ounces, but not to me. Everyone tells me that will change if I become a grandparent, and I believe it. I'm sure I'll be more protective and involved when the baby is related to me.

In the human model, we refer to "deadbeat dads" or "absentee parents"—those who are involved in the reproduction and conception phases, but then leave and build no discernible relationship with their offspring. With parent/daughter churches this can happen for a number of reasons. One reason may be the abrupt departure of the senior leadership of the parent church. Vision should be owned by the church at large, but more than that it is owned by the senior leadership (pastor and key board members). If the original visionaries move on, the parent church may move into a survival role in which nurturing a daughter church becomes a low priority. Another factor leading to the neglect of daughter churches is jealousy, causing constituent backlash. If the new church exudes fast growth and excitement, it's possible for senior leadership at the parent church to feel competitive, resulting in neglect. Sometimes church members may begin to complain that "all we ever do around here is talk about the new church." Backlash can quiet leadership, which can lead to neglect.

Principles of Healthy Parenting/Daughter Church Relationships

As with most things in life, inter-church relationships depend on leadership. In a real sense, "churches" don't relate to each other, people do. As long as the leaders of the parent church proactively relate to the daughter church leadership, the landmine of neglect can be avoided. Some principles:

Principle # 1:
> The role of the parent decreases over time, and the parent church needs to accept that. Hopefully, there will always be a meaningful relationship between parent and daughter churches, but the parent has the most influence during the conception phase. Daughter churches should strive for independence. An extrapolated period of dependence is not healthy.

Principle # 2:
> Have written agreements ahead of time. In our movement (Converge Worldwide) it is standard operating procedure to have soon-to-be-deployed church planters submit a "Project Proposal" which outlines the model, timeline, target community, and all other relevant details that can be put on paper. This document is negotiated and then approved by the sending agency so there are as few surprises as possible. Church plants also sit down for an "Expectations Interview," where every denominational policy, doctrinal distinctive, and procedure is explained and initialed. This limits misunderstandings that are endemic to new ventures and provides an objective anchor to come back to in times of confusion.

Principle #3:
> The senior pastor of the parent church must praise, defend, and encourage the daughter church. When churches plant churches, there will always be detractors who resist the idea or the process. No one can speak more forthrightly to this than the senior pastor, who in a sense, serves as the lightning rod for backlash. Alternative opinions can be heard, but once the course is set and agreed to, objections will need to be addressed firmly and with maturity. The pastor can celebrate and praise the new work in private conversations, publicly, and through written communiqués. Similarly, the pastor of the new work will want to maintain a posture of goodwill and appreciation in public references to the parent church.

Principle # 4:
> Occasional connecting events can deepen the corporate mission. Early on, the parent church can host special events, such as a baby shower, to bless

the new church with materials and equipment for getting started. As the church grows, jointly held celebrations (such as baptisms, holiday services, etc.) can be considered. Each church will be autonomous, but each can extend its hand of fellowship for the sake of celebration and mission.

Failure to Recover

My wife Lori reluctantly ventured into motherhood. I'll never forget her response after our first son was born. Despite a night of agonizing labor she exclaimed, "I could do that again!" So she did – but not immediately.

It takes time to recover! Giving birth isn't easy for mothers or for mother churches. Even when the church multiplication flame burns strong, wise leaders anticipate the need to regroup before the church intentionally starts to do it again. You may have heard stories of a parent church sending a group of people away, and by the following week they have fully recovered their attendance and offerings. That's great. Jesus did teach, "Give, and it will be given to you. A good measure, pressed down, shaken together and running over, will be poured into your lap. For with the measure you use, it will be measured to you (Luke 6:38)." So we encourage generosity and sacrifice – but we also encourage wisdom.

The stories of instant recovery are real, but they are also the headline-grabbers which are the exception rather than the rule. Most of us need to take measured, healthy approaches in order to have a perpetuating record of church planting success. Jesus also said, "Suppose one of you wants to build a tower. Will he not first sit down and estimate the cost to see if he has enough money to complete it?" (Luke 14:28). Prudence is just as much a biblical virtue as sacrifice is.

It's hard to improve on Bob Logan and Steve Ogne's list of six recovery needs for a parent church (*Churches Planting Churches*, p. 12-16). A brief look at them follows:

Physically: In many cases, the membership of a parent church becomes physically invested in the planting of a daughter church. There is equipment to acquire or refurbish. There are endless meetings and logistical arrangements. Because this can be exhausting, call for a season of rest. A church could even call for a moratorium on meetings for a while. God's antidote to Elijah following the confrontation with the prophets of Baal was to rest, eat, and recover (I Kings 19:5-8).

Emotionally: In human birth, "postpartum" is a depression that takes place following the much-anticipated birthing event. One of my church planting heroes is Dr. Dan Maxton, who has led several churches to reproduce themselves. He says, "The grand opening of a church is like the birth of a child and the marriage of that child all in the same day!" It's like a baby and a sibling all in one. Some friendships are now altered forever. Things won't ever be the same. Some solace is found in rejoicing that the new congregation is off and running, but some emotional recovery just takes time for processing. Leaders need to remind the church that the emotional hit is real, but in the end it is worth it.

Financially: There is a financial price to pay for giving birth. In most cases the parent church is allocating start-up funds and the entire congregation pitches in to some degree. But when a core group of people leaves the parent church to launch the new church, many of them represent faithful giving units. Churches build their budgets with more and deeper pockets. After birth the parent church has fewer pockets. It's all part of the sacrifice. Prepare for this by increasing reserves ahead of time and reminding the congregation of that reality.

Attendance loss: Depending on the church planting model employed, parent churches can either experience a subtle attendance loss, or a dramatic exodus. Both the parent and the plant may notice attendance fluctuation. Many who leave to help the new church will return to their more natural church setting within a year. Some members may leave permanently. Except for large churches, some degree of attendance depletion will be felt. If the church is healthy, it will recover. However, it could take a year or more. Planning intentional outreach emphases at the right time will remind the church that its daughter isn't the only show in town.

Leadership loss: One of the payoffs for planting daughter churches is that new leaders will, of necessity, be raised up in the parent church. That's good, but it's also a double-edged sword, because for a season the church will need to recover its leadership base as well. The operative principle here is for the parent church to prepare in advance and not be shocked when some good leaders move on. During the conception and pre-natal phases, intentional apprenticing can offset the possible shock to come. But the loss of leadership leaves a residual effect in the parent church that takes time to overcome.

Vision depletion: The King James Version of the Bible translates Proverbs 29:18 as "Where there is no vision, the people perish." Part of recovery involves dreaming again, and maybe dreaming bigger than before. I'll say more on this at the end of the chapter.

Three Axioms

I've often said that things look better in books than in real life, and the issue of parent church recovery is a prime example. We thank God for the stories of those churches that are blessed with instant recovery, but remember to apply wisdom and anticipate an intentional recovery season for your church when you start a daughter congregation. Planting churches requires sacrifice, and we need you to be healthy for the long-term! Keep in mind these three axioms for recovery:

1. The smaller the church, the more likely your need for an intentional and protracted recovery plan.

2. The more people you send, the greater your need for recovery. Not all church planting models have the same impact on a parent church, so plan accordingly.

3. The less experienced a church is in reproducing itself, the greater the need for recovery. Once reproduction becomes systematic, recovery will be as well.

Reflecting on a successful church birth in Eau Claire, Wisconsin, Dan Maxton writes with the wisdom of experience. "After parenting Valleybrook Church there was an initial flood of joy and satisfaction in seeing our new baby church getting started. Then grief replaced joy as we more fully realized that our friendships and relationships would never be the same again with those leaders and people who had left. I wished I had had the foresight to plan for the next stage of our own growth and outreach for us, the mother church. Parenting was not the finish line, it was really just the starting line."

Intentional Infertility

What if parenting a new church really isn't the finish line? What if it really is just the starting line?

I'm a fan of Garrison Keillor and his *Prairie Home Companion*. His stories center in a fictional town called Lake Wobegon, the "gateway to central Minnesota". Inhabited by a quirky populace of Catholic and Lutheran blue-collar townsfolk and farmers, Lake Wobegon lives by the motto: "Sumus quod sumus," which means "We are what we are." That might be their current reality, but it's no vision statement of what they can become!

Churches that choose to reproduce themselves are in effect saying, "We're not going to be what we've always been. We're going to be more than that!" With all of the landmines associated with parenting churches, you might wonder why any church would choose to reproduce. But standing still is a much greater risk than venturing into something new. The landmine of doing nothing is more perilous than the landmine of moving ahead.

At the risk of exhausting the proud parent church, there is something to be said for striking while the iron's hot. Certain seasons are more fertile than others. For instance, I've noticed that even the most prolific planting churches often shelve their commitment to church reproduction once the original visionary pastor moves on. Few pastoral candidates overtly oppose church planting, but few will continue to lead the church to reproduce. So, there are seasons of fertility where a church should consider moving from a church planting "event" mentality (parenting one church) to a church planting "culture" mentality (which assumes that reproduction is the expected norm).

How can a church accomplish this? Begin with the end in mind. If parenting isn't the finish line, but the starting line, there's a lot of opportunity for expansion. One pastor held an apple before his congregation and said, "I don't know what you see here, but I see a grove of apple trees as far as the eye can see." With church parenting experience, visionary plans gain more credibility. Imagine and plan for a family of churches. Intentionality, not hype (which normally backfires), in developing faith goals and action plans can set your church on course. Keep your eye on the harvest. Continue to study your ministry area and continue to pray for the lost. Demographics are always shifting. Enlist volunteers to continue making you aware of the needs. One pastor, at a standstill moment in his church's history, loaded the congregation into buses on a Sunday morning and drove them through the city so they could become aware of local opportunities. Another church used their youth group to do the demographic research, prayer walks, and door-to-door work to determine their next church planting site.

Keep yourselves inspired. Attend church planting conferences, and bring key leaders (including opinion leaders) along. Create a local church planting gathering to share your experiences with others. Invite church planters to address your congregation. Offer internships. And continue to invite people from your church to consider the church planting venture.

Pray. Continue to ask God what steps to take next. Cultivate a sense of spiritual dependence, constantly alerting people to pray. Open a map before your congregation and prayer groups and ask them to consider the opportunities before them. On occasion, call the church to fast.

Consider a new model or target group. If you know how to do one thing well, don't neglect that, but consider other ways to expand your missional capacity. Now may be the time to target a different ethnic group or an under-reached age group. Who isn't being reached by the churches in this community? If your first daughter was a classic church plant, perhaps this next one will be a multi-site or pre-autonomous church.

Broaden your partnerships. Who else can help you plant this next church? Are there sister, aunt, and uncle churches who would thrive with the opportunity to participate. Ask other churches what they can do in terms of the "three P's": prayer, people (experts, short-term missionaries, launch team members), and purse.

Final Thoughts

I give the final word to my friend, Dr. Dan Maxton. Dan says:

> Looking back over my years of parenting churches these are lessons that I've learned: (1) Release families and share resources generously. Take to heart Proverbs 11:24, "One man gives freely, yet gains even more; another withholds unduly, but comes to poverty ... he who refreshes others will himself be refreshed;" (2) Never expect a perfect time to parent; resist the "good" reasons to delay or abandon your parenting dreams; (3) Cast vision for parenting with courage. Treat dissenters, skeptics and critics with respect, but don't allow them to derail your vision; (4) Launching a daughter church is only the starting line, not the finish line. Plan for the recovery and future ministry plans of the parent church before you give birth, not after.

Questions to consider while navigating the landmine of after-birth neglect:
- How will you avoid hype while discovering and casting true vision to plant churches?
- How will you prepare your church for postpartum loss?
- Do you agree that parenting is the starting line, not the finish line? How does this impact your next steps?

Recommended Resources:
- *Five Things Anyone Can Do to Help Plant a Church*, by Phil Stevenson, Wesleyan Publishing House, 2008

Preparing to Parent Values Assessment

T he following is a qualitative assessment of congregational readiness to birth a new church. While birthing potential is latent in most any context, this tool is intended to assess and call attention to the values that tend to support the parenting of new churches.

Answer each question according to the following scale:

0	1	2	3

NEVER------------RARELY--------------SOMETIMES-------------OFTEN

1. Our church is characterized by investing resources into the lives of people who are not members.
2. Our ministry style is one that outsiders can quickly relate to.
3. Our church is often taking on new methods to share the good news of Jesus.
4. We have a history of raising up new leaders for ministry.
5. Our congregation has a pattern of making bold plans that depend on God's provision.
6. Leadership at our church seems to care less about who gets the credit as long as the job gets done.
7. We have a giving community. We often take up funds for those outside our ministry.
8. Our church has ministries outside our walls where the message and presence of Jesus is shared.
9. The teaching of our church engages seekers and speaks to their needs.

10. Our leadership often reminds us of the number of people yet to be reached in our community.
11. We have watched with joy as some of our best leaders move on to new ministry opportunities.
12. Our church has often had to rely entirely on God to reach its goals.
13. Our congregation has partnered with other denominations to do effective ministry.
14. We have committed funds to help plant new ministries outside our walls.
15. Our congregation has mobilized to meet significant needs in the community.
16. The worship of our church is led in a way that engages seekers and speaks to their needs.
17. Our church never lets money stand in the way of making new disciples.
18. There is a "leadership pathway" at church whereby new leaders are mentored and trained.
19. We dream God sized dreams and worry about the resources later.
20. Our congregation is focused on people being followers of Christ, not on what denomination they are part of.
21. Our congregation has recruited funds and people to help start a new church.
22. We have a portion of our church budget that is devoted to making a caring impact on the community around us.
23. Our congregation is connected to the community needs around us in ways that are well received by outsiders.
24. We have a culture where making new disciples is expected and planned for.
25. Our pastors and staff are often empowering younger leaders and encouraging their development.
26. Our congregation has stories of how God met needs beyond our dreams.
27. We are not easily threatened by new church starts nearby.
28. Our church has a history of reaching funding goals for outreach efforts.
29. Our leadership gives considerable time to discern and strategize how to show the love of Christ to our community.
30. I have noticed dimensions of our ministry that attract new people.
31. In the last year there has been at least one class or sermon series on how to share our faith winsomely.
32. Our church has a ministry in identifying, training and releasing new ministry leaders.
33. We trust that where God leads, God provides.
34. Our leadership has an abundance mentality as far as ministry opportunities are concerned.

35. We maintain a percentage of our church budget that is committed for mission type efforts.

ANSWERS:

I.	II.	III.	IV.	V.	VI.	VII.

1._____ 2._____ 3._____ 4._____ 5._____ 6._____ 7._____

8._____ 9._____ 10._____ 11._____ 12._____ 13._____ 14._____

15._____ 16._____ 17_____ 18._____ 19._____ 20._____ 21._____

22._____ 23._____ 24._____ 25._____ 26._____ 27._____ 28._____

29._____ 30._____ 31._____ 32._____ 33._____ 34._____ 35._____

TOTALS FROM COLUMNS and PARENTING VALUES THEY REPRESENT

I._____ COMPASSION FOR THE UNCHURCHED: cares enough about lost people that significant amounts of time, energy and resources are invested to reach them.

II._____ CULTURALLY RELEVANT STYLE: utilizes a style of ministry that attracts seekers and addresses their needs.

III._____ GREAT COMMISSION ORIENTATION: sees ministry potential in terms of limitations of facilities and/or finances. Committed to make disciples and multiply.

IV._____ DEVELOPING AND RELEASING LEADERS: activly seeks to train and/or mentor potential planters; encourages giving away the best leaders to start new churches.

V. _____ CONFIDENCE IN GOD'S ABILITY: makes bold plans for the future, recognizing that our faith rests in God's resources and not our own.

VI._____ KINGDOM PERSPECTIVE: encouraging new churches to start nearby even if it takes away from the local ministry. Views the total harvest to be important.

VII._____ GENEROSITY: healthy churches will give people financial resources freely to help get new churches started.

TOTAL SCORE: _____

SCORING SCALE:

85-105   Your church is likely to be a good candidate to parent a new church having established the essential values in your culture to support the vision.

70-84   Your congregation is on its way to parenting as you are becoming familiar with the values that support church planting.

55-69   Your congregation is early in the process of becoming a multiplying culture. Identifying a couple values to improve is your next step.

0-54   Your ministry is exploring a major shift in values as you consider parenting. Working on one area at a time is your next step.

*   This assessment is based on the "Values of Healthy Parent Churches" as found in *Churches Planting Churches* by Robert E. Logan and Steven L. Ogne, Published by Church Smart Resources, 1995.

Great Lakes Region RCA
Ben Ingebretson 10/08

Appendix B
Sample Planter/Parent Covenant

"....so that the sower and the reaper may be glad together."
— John 4: 36

I. Commitments of the Parent Congregation to the Planter

    a. We will support this effort with prayer and advocacy by: _____

_____

    b. We will keep communication open and healthy by:_____

_____

    c. We will commit these resources:_____

_____

    d. We will seek to build trust by:_____

_____

    e. Other:_____

II. Commitments of the Planter to the Parent Congregation

   a. I will keep communication open and healthy by:_____

_____

   b. I will be accountable by:_____

_____

   c. I will seek to build trust by:_____

_____

   d. I will honor the support of the parent by:_____

_____

   e. Other:_____

III. Shared Commitments in Decision Making Relative to:

   a. The primary objective, target and purpose of the plant :
      As parent and planter we commit together to maintain the original intent
      and purpose of this plant unless we agree otherwise.

   b. The fiscal sustainability of the new church plant:
      As parent and planter we commit to a financial plan and budget that is ap-
      propriate and agreeable to both parties.

   c. Staffing evaluation, additions and eliminations in the new church plant:
      As parent and planter we commit to staffing decisions and evaluation that
      are a result of due process and shared understanding.

   d. We agree to meet monthly to review progress and our shared
      commitments.

Signatures of Parent Congregation leadership and Planter:

_____ & _____

Appendix C

Sample Expectations Interview

GREAT LAKES
CHURCH PLANTING
EXPECTATIONS INTERVIEW

Revised, June 2005

Church Planter:_____

Interviewed by:_____ Date:_____

Purpose: The purpose of this Expectations Interview is to assure that the lines of communication are clear between the Great Lakes Baptist Conference (GLBC) and its church planters regarding policies and procedures during the church planting process.

**Great Lakes Church Planters May Expect the Following
from the Great Lakes Baptist Conference
(To be initialed by a representative of Great Lakes Church Planting)**

_____You will be honored in spirit and in practice. Those in leadership will treat you with dignity both in public and private conversations.

_____You will be coached by experienced personnel. You will be met face-to-face each month through the first anniversary of your public launch, and to a lesser degree thereafter. You will be routinely contacted by e-mail and telephone.

_____Your spouse will be supported through networking opportunities, phone calls, e-mail, and occasional special events.

_____The GLBC will provide a support-raising coach and funding for support-raising costs.

_____The GLBC will provide financial resources according to your call package. You will be reimbursed promptly for expenses submitted at the end of each month.

_____Great Lakes Church Planting church planters are part of the GLBC "family," and as such, they may avail themselves of all of the resources of the GLBC.

_____The GLBC will provide training through special conferences, retreats, and other occasional events.

_____The GLBC will supply resources for pulpit supply, special speakers, and pastoral retreat and vacation help for you and your family.

_____At GLBC expense, you will enjoy the benefits of being part of a regional LEAD Team whose aim is to provide mutual encouragement and strategic support for its members.

_____In the event that your church planting venture does not succeed, the GLBC will recommend you for other ministry opportunities as appropriate.

_____Representatives of GLBC ministries will be available to meet with your church board to offer guidance with formulating a budget, sabbatical and personnel policies, and other procedural matters.

_____The spirit of the GLBC is to help meet your needs, to the degree that we can, in order to help you succeed in your mission. The GLBC Church Planting Committee will regularly pray for you and your needs.

**The Great Lakes Baptist Conference May Expect the Following
from Each Great Lakes Church Planter
(To be initialed by the church planter)**

Area 1: Movement Issues

_____ I understand that this is a movement of new church planting, and I will play a part in seeing new churches start beyond my own ministry location.

_____ I have read and will abide by the Advertising Policy of Great Lakes Church Planting.

_____ In keeping with the values of the Great Lakes Church Planting movement, I will, as of day one, become part of a regional LEAD team, as assigned.

_____ My spouse will participate in LEADnet or its equivalent.

_____ I agree to be coached by a member of the Great Lakes Church Planting Coaching Staff, as assigned. My Coach will serve as my primary, though not exclusive, resource person.

_____ Both my spouse and I will have e-mail addresses, and we will check e-mail regularly.

_____ If I do not qualify for any of the pre-stated exceptions, I will enroll and participate in the GLBC Health Insurance Program.

_____ During our new church's "Pre-Natal" phase, I will invite representatives of the Great Lakes Church Planting movement (my coach, the Director of Church Planting, or the District Executive Minister, etc.) to meet with our launch team for the purpose of establishing a sound relationship.

_____ Our church will initially adopt the standard "GLBC Church Constitution" as its constitution, understanding that it may be amended as our church matures.

_____ My coach and I will communicate the content of this Expectations Interview with the leadership of my church plant.

Area 2: District and Denominational Cooperation

_____ I will lead my church with the intention of affiliating as a member church with the Great Lakes Baptist Conference and the Baptist General Conference. Within three months of arrival on site, I will contact the Chairman of the GLBC Affiliation Council and the District Executive Minister to initiate the Affiliation process.

_____ I will attend the Annual Meeting of the GLBC in October of each year.

_____ Both my spouse and I will attend the annual One Mission Retreat.

_____ Both my spouse and I will attend the "New Pastors' Orientation" at the GLBC Service Center or at a satellite location some time during the first year of our ministry.

_____ Some time during the first year of public ministry, representatives from my church will attend the "Do It Right" financial seminar at the GLBC Service Center (or at a satellite location).

_____ I will cooperate with the GLBC Service Center by providing mailing lists, email lists, and other informational requests relative to our church.

_____ Our church will supply, when asked, testimonies and anecdotal information to the GLBC for promotional purposes.

_____ Our church will maintain a posture of positive cooperation with the GLBC, seeking mutual encouragement and enhancement of ministry.

_____ Within the first three months of ministry, I will arrange for a personal interview with the District Executive Minister.

Area 3: Character Development and Spiritual Issues

_____ I will develop a personal Intercession Team (see *The Church Planter's Toolkit*, Chapter 2) and communicate regularly with them.

_____ I will communicate honestly with my Coach and with the broader movement of the GLBC.

_____ I have read and will abide by the "BGC Ministerial Code of Ethics".

_____ I will take at least one day off from ministry per week.

_____ We will take at least one week of vacation annually.

Area 4: Financial Issues

_____ Before beginning support-raising I will meet with my support-raising coach and submit to the process.

_____ I understand that certain GLBC churches may support me financially. I will pursue these churches according to the directives of the Great Lakes Church Planting office and the GLBC.

_____ It is my understanding that the Internal Revenue Service requires that excess funds which remain in my account at the conclusion of my support agreement with the GLBC are owned and directed by the GLBC, and will be diverted to other church planting efforts.

_____ From the time we begin to receive offerings we will tithe at least 10% from our church income to the ministries of the Baptist General Conference and the Great Lakes Baptist Conference. The tithe will be distributed according to current GLBC policy and will include portions for the Baptist General Conference (undesignated), the Great Lakes Baptist Conference (undesignated), my LEAD Team work funds, and general church planting work funds.

_____ Following our affiliation with the GLBC and reaching self-supporting status our church will continue to give at least 10% of its income to GLBC and BGC ministries.

_____ While receiving financial or administrative help (receipting, coaching, etc.) from the GLBC, our church will not contribute financially to any other mission agency outside of the Baptist General Conference.

_____ I will submit reimbursements at the end of each month in an orderly and accurate manner. During August, I will make sure such reimbursements reach the GLBC Service Center prior to the end of the month (and fiscal year).

_____ Following the public launch of our church, we will submit quarterly financial reports to the GLBC bookkeeping department for two years. This is to assure quality control and compliance with normal tax law and standardized reporting procedures.

_____ I understand that there is a 5% administrative fee which the GLBC will take from my salary account to help defray the costs of receipting gifts donated on my behalf. I understand that this fee does not cover the entire cost of the GLBC's service in this area. This fee percentage may change on occasion.

_____ When salary support is no longer needed I will work with the GLBC to invite my donors to consider other church planting projects to transition their support toward.

Area 5: Doctrinal Issues

_____ I have read and accept the "Affirmation of Faith" of the Baptist General Conference, which will serve as the theological base of our new church.

_____ In keeping with the current policy of the GLBC, our church will accept into its formal membership only believers who have been baptized by immersion.

_____ As a church, we will practice the Lord's Supper regularly.

Area 6: Termination

_____ I understand that my position as a church planter with the GLBC may be terminated under, though not limited to, the following conditions:

1. Moral failure.
2. Church leadership request or the congregational vote to remove me as pastor of the church.
3. A perpetual unteachable attitude and/or routine failure to live up to my commitments with the GLBC.

_____ Should my church dissolve its affiliation/relationship with the BGC and/or the GLBC, the GLBC has the right to request and receive full reimbursement for any District moneys and services dispensed during the formation of the church.

Great Lakes Church Planting Representative   Date

Great Lakes Church Planting Church Planter   Date

Great Lakes Church Planting Spouse   Date

AREAS OF DISAGREEMENT, CLARIFICATION, OR OTHER
DISCUSSION:

Signature of Church Planter:_____

Church Planting Mobilization Risk Factor Analysis

Church planter_____ Date_____

Church planting is a risky business, but experience shows that when a qualified church planter is fitted with the right environmental situation the likelihood of success is greatly enhanced. The following guide is to help you, the potential church planter, determine whether now is the right time and this is the right place for you to enter into the arena of church planting.

For the following, circle the number on each line which best represents your situation:

How will you be personally funded?

```
1-------------------2---------------------3-------------------4----------------------5
```
faith   bi-vocational   partial support   spouse/   fully funded
                                                     strong support

Does the site selection match your cultural background or experience?

```
1-------------------2---------------------3-------------------4--------------------5
```
not really   a little   moderately   pretty much   absolutely

How many ministry partners will move with you?

```
1--------------------2--------------------3-----------------------4------------------5
none            1 or 2              3 or 4               5 or 6              7 or 8
```

How many pre-existing adult contacts (individuals or couples) that you already know or are aware of, might likely become part of your team?

```
1--------------------2--------------------3--------------------4--------------------5
none            1 or 2              3 or 4               5 or 6              7 or 8
```

How near is your family or your spouse's family or natural support group?

```
1-----------------------------------2-------------------------------3
would take           within driving distance          nearby
an airplane          for a weekend visit.
```

How closely does your ministry site approximate your geographic roots?

```
1-----------------------------------2-------------------------------3
not much             somewhat              quite a bit
```

How close are you to other supportive churches who really want you to succeed?

```
1-----------------------------------2-------------------------------3
not close at all        somewhat            very close
```

How much vocational ministry success have you personally experienced?

```
1-----------------------------------2-------------------------------3
none so far             a little              a lot
```

Scoring

Now total your score, and compare it to the general guidelines below.

8-15 HIGH RISK: As a qualified church planter you will seriously need to consider whether this is the right time and/or the right place to church plant. Prayerfully discuss this with district personnel who may be able to point you to less risky opportunities or help you to re-engineer your time line.

16-23 MODERATE RISK: As a qualified church planter, you need to realize that this will be a challenging experience. Bring this decision before the Lord and others experienced in church planting. If God's calling seems clear, proceed with conviction and wisdom. If there is strong uncertainty, district personnel may be able to point you to less risky opportunities or help you to re-engineer your time line. Remember: some risk is normal. The Great Commission does not call us to avoid challenging situations!

24-32 LOW RISK: As a qualified church planter, the environmental issues here seem to point toward a positive church planting experience. There will still be challenges, of course. You must prayerfully consider God's leading in this venture. If he so leads, you will likely find success.

My numerical score_____

My risk category_____

Other thoughts and/or action steps:

Start Coaching in Ten Minutes!

Coaching is the hands-on process of helping someone to succeed. In my view, it relates to both discipleship and mentoring, but in its own unique way. In discipleship, the leader sets the agenda, deciding which topics will be pursued. In mentoring, the follower (protégé) sets the agenda, coming to the mentor as needed. Coaching is sort of a combination of both discipleship and mentoring. The coach has a specific agenda to pursue, but he or she pursues this agenda according to the unique needs and circumstances of the one being coached. Consider this matrix:

Methodology	Agenda	Posture of Leader	Posture of Follower
Discipleship	Set by leader	Pursues follower	Receives instruction
Mentoring	Set by follower	Is available as needed	Pursues leader when needed
Coaching	Set by both	Pursues follower	Pursues leader

Likely you've had a variety of good coaches throughout your life: a teacher, a Boy or Girl Scout leader, a piano teacher, an athletic coach, a Sunday school teacher, or a pastor. Likewise, you've coached many people in one way or another.

Coaches help us get more out of ourselves than we would naturally realize. The Bible says, "As iron sharpens iron, so one person sharpens another" (Proverbs 27:17). And, "Let us consider how we may spur one another on toward love and good deeds" (Hebrews 10:24). Our effectiveness increases and our contribution broadens with good coaching. Accordingly, when we learn to coach others well, we make an even more significant kingdom impact by helping others reach their potential.

Qualities of Good Coaches

Good coaches display a number of qualities:
- They listen actively, gathering good information without being consumed with autobiographical listening (telling their own story).
- They care personally—both for the personal life and the ministry progress.
- They focus on developing character, helping the follower grasp God's perspective and priorities.
- They encourage excellence, not settling for mediocrity.
- They push perseverance, helping the follower to gain the resolve to keep moving amidst hardship.
- They help in problem-solving, raising options and pointing followers toward resources.
- They hold followers accountable to complete assignments and achieve goals.
- They celebrate wins, making sure that followers enjoy the satisfaction of having been used well by God.

Your Two Best Coaching Tools

Coaching is a multifaceted art. As you learn a few techniques, you'll be positioned to use this methodology in a variety of settings: at home, at work, in ministry ... everywhere! Though coaching is profound in what it can deliver, it's relatively simple in terms of technique. If you'll learn two acronyms and implement what they stand for, you'll be well on your way toward coaching success.

The First Acronym: WAIT — WAIT means Why Am I Talking? Surprisingly to some, coaching is not about continual advice-giving. Rather, it has more to do with helping another achieve self-discovery—and holding him or her accountable to perform the action-points he or she commits to. So the first rule of coaching is that we're more about *listening* than *talking*. Internally we do our best to hold our tongues. (Why am I talking, anyway? I should be listening!) In fact, there are two sub-strategies for achieving WAIT.

The first sub-strategy is to listen empathetically. That means we listen to gather information, but it also means we truly attempt to get inside the thinking of the other. Stephen Covey, in his landmark book *Seven Habits of Highly Effective People*, says that we must "diagnose before we prescribe." He uses the analogy of going to an optometrist to have poor eyesight corrected. What if rather than making a careful diagnosis to determine the prescription needed, the optometrist handed you his glasses and told you to wear them? That would constitute major malpractice. You wouldn't have been cared for and you couldn't see any better—maybe even worse—than before.

A good coach listens empathetically. So, try to not over-tell your stories. Try not to engage in "autobiographical listening." (Can you think of a time when your back hurt, and everyone around you started to tell their backache stories? How fun was that?!) A good coach curbs telling his or her stories in order to listen to others and help them come up with helpful strategies.

The second sub-strategy is to ask good questions. When coaching, try to have at least 75% of what comes out of your mouth come in the form of a question. Much of your best teaching will come in the form of questions. Think of how many times Jesus taught with questions. Then think of the good questions you've been asked.

Questions not only keep you from talking too much, they also help the other toward greater self-discovery. You can find many good resources to help you learn to ask good questions. Remember one of the basics is: Don't ask too many closed-ended questions which can be answered with a yes or no.

The Second Acronym: GROW — GROW is a template—a coaching guide—to tackle a coaching issue. It suggests the four phases involved when coaching someone: (1) Goal definition, (2) Reality assessment, (3) Options considered, and (4) Will do something. Keep saying those words: Goal, Reality, Options, Will. Think of the template as an arrow or a funnel, moving another toward the target or the resolution of an issue.

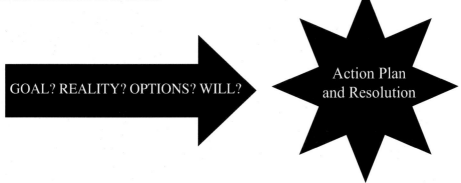

GOAL? REALITY? OPTIONS? WILL?

Action Plan and Resolution

For example, say a person you're coaching needs to discuss how to recruit more children's workers for the Sunday school program. Ask, "What is your goal?" The answer may be simple: "To recruit six more Sunday school workers." The situation, however, may be more complex than that.

So once the goal is defined, ask something such as, "What is the current reality? How have you recruited workers in the past? What's worked? What's not worked? Is the pastor helpful?" Such questions squarely force describing current reality in context. This is the "diagnose before you prescribe" phase.

Understanding the context, you're set to move on to considering Options. "What options do you have?" (Note you're asking for more than one.) Keep probing for more and more options; you may add a few yourself. You could help the person discover a dozen options. This is good. Hope is on the way.

Finally, how do you close the deal? Ask, "Considering these options, which will you implement? What *Will* you do?" The one you're coaching will eventually agree to certain action steps. You may need to challenge the person to do more— or maybe less. You're the coach.

Remember this axiom: **Coaching hasn't happened until an action plan has been agreed to**. And remember this axiom: **the one being coached does the work!**

Your job then is to help hold the person accountable. You may say, "May I call you next Wednesday to see if you've met with the pastor yet?" Or, "Will you send me a copy of the letter you will be sending by next Tuesday?" Notice how specifically and time-bound you're holding the person accountable. By the way, accountability is the reason you'll want to take notes to record agreements and action plans. Generally you won't need to be hard on the person. Agreement to an action plan and willingness to be held accountable will produce enormous results.

You'll have more to learn as you aim to increase your coaching proficiency, but these coaching basics will get you on your way. Go for it, and trust the Holy Spirit to use you as you "spur one another on."

Agenda/Values Survey

Name_____

This is a survey to help us discern how compatible you may be with the direction of The Crossing Church Plant. Please record your views as accurately as possible, not what you think someone might want you to say. Read each statement and indicate if it would be a high priority, low priority, or somewhere in between. If you feel any form of explanation is needed for your response, please star that statement and include your notes on the back of the page. Please note that while some of these statements may seem to be mutually-exclusive (i.e. contemporary v. traditional music), that is not necessarily the case. You are not limited to a certain amount of "High Priorities".

	High Priority			Low Priority

1. Significant variety in the church service

$$1 - 2 - 3 - 4 - 5$$

2. A highly relational senior pastor

$$1 - 2 - 3 - 4 - 5$$

3. A worship service that would relate to the unchurched

$$1 - 2 - 3 - 4 - 5$$

4. Singing traditional hymns

$$1 - 2 - 3 - 4 - 5$$

	High Priority				Low Priority

5. A pastor who is a gifted communicator

1 – 2 – 3 – 4 – 5

6. Public meetings (worship services) presented with excellence

1 – 2 – 3 – 4 – 5

7. A church open to stylistic innovation and change

1 – 2 – 3 – 4 – 5

8. Being able to use my gifts to strengthen the church body

1   2   3   4   5

9. Women serving as elders

1 – 2 – 3 – 4 – 5

10. Elders setting the course and providing leadership

1 – 2 – 3 – 4 – 5

11. Significant giving to missions

1 – 2 – 3 – 4 – 5

12. Birthing additional churches from our own

1 – 2 – 3 – 4 – 5

13. Singing contemporary worship music

1 – 2 – 3 – 4 – 5

14. Meeting local community needs

1 – 2 – 3 – 4 – 5

15. Adult discipleship classes

1 – 2 – 3 – 4 – 5

16. One-on-one mentoring relationships

1 – 2 – 3 – 4 – 5

17. Quality children's ministry

1 – 2 – 3 – 4 – 5

High Priority   Low Priority

18. Quality youth ministry

1 – 2 – 3 – 4 – 5

19. A pastor who regularly visits people's homes

1 – 2 – 3 – 4 – 5

20. Small group ministry

1 – 2 – 3 – 4 – 5

21. A pastor available for personal counseling

1 – 2 – 3 – 4 – 5

22. An active women's ministry

1 – 2 – 3 – 4 – 5

23. An active men's ministry

1 – 2 – 3 – 4 – 5

24. The opportunity to speak in tongues during a worship service

1 – 2 – 3 – 4 – 5

25. Expressive worship

1 – 2 – 3 – 4 – 5

26. In-depth, verse-by-verse teaching during the worship service

1 – 2 – 3 – 4 – 5

27. Sermons that would connect with my unchurched friends

1 – 2 – 3 – 4 – 5

28. A church that encourages formal attire

1 – 2 – 3 – 4 – 5

29. An orderly and traditional worship service

1 – 2 – 3 – 4 – 5

30. An informal, cutting edge worship service

1 – 2 – 3 – 4 – 5

| | High Priority | Low Priority |

31. A congregation consistently growing in size

1 – 2 – 3 – 4 – 5

32. A church that effectively trains people for ministry

1 – 2 – 3 – 4 – 5

33. A church with strong pastoral leadership

1 – 2 – 3 – 4 – 5

34. Slow change rather than rapid change

1 – 2 – 3 – 4 – 5

35. A church that plans and sets goals

1 – 2 – 3 – 4 – 5

36. Church leaders who never hurt or offend anyone

1 – 2 – 3 – 4 – 5

37. A pastor serving as head elder

1 – 2 – 3 – 4 – 5

38. A church that is action-oriented

1 – 2 – 3 – 4 – 5

39. A church that is prayer-oriented

1 – 2 – 3 – 4 – 5

40. A church intent on building up believers

1 – 2 – 3 – 4 – 5

41. A church intent on reaching the lost

1 – 2 – 3 – 4 – 5

42. A church with a lecture format for teaching/learning

1 – 2 – 3 – 4 – 5

43. A church with interaction and discovery for teaching/learning

1 – 2 – 3 – 4 – 5

High Priority   Low Priority

44. A church where everyone has input regarding decisions

1 – 2 – 3 – 4 – 5

45. A church with strong leadership that sets the direction

1 – 2 – 3 – 4 – 5

46. Training classes for new believers

1 – 2 – 3 – 4 – 5

47. A church assisting parents in Christian education and formation

1 – 2 – 3 – 4 – 5

48. A church that takes responsibility for Christian Ed. and formation

1 – 2 – 3 – 4 – 5

49. A worship band / team

1 – 2 – 3 – 4 – 5

50. A church that practices a Biblical pattern of church discipline

1 – 2 – 3 – 4 – 5

51. Man has free will

1 – 2 – 3 – 4 – 5

52. A pastor who teaches the pre-tribulation rapture

1 – 2 – 3 – 4 – 5

53. A pastor who spends most of his time with people

1 – 2 – 3 – 4 – 5

54. A pastor who spends most of his time in his study

1 – 2 – 3 – 4 – 5

55. A pastor who spends most of his time on the golf course

1 – 2 – 3 – 4 – 5

Choose five (5) items that are MOST IMPORTANT to you. Rank them in order of priority (Highest=1). Yes, all are important, but choose only five.

___Teaching the Bible   ___Community/Small Groups
___Addressing social causes   ___Music/Praise
___Discipleship/training believers   ___Missions
___Administration (finances, buildings, etc.)   ___Evangelism
___Counseling/pastoral care   ___Prayer
___Assimilating new people   ___Planning and goals
___Ministry to youth   ___Ministry to children

Read each statement below and respond with one of the following numbers:
        1 …….. I believe that strongly
        2……… I believe that
        3……… I'm uncertain
        4……… I don't believe that
        5……… I know that isn't true

1. The Bible is the inspired Word of God.   _____
2. The Bible is without error.   _____
3. The Bible is the ultimate authority for my life.   _____
4. Jesus is the Son of God.   _____
5. Jesus is God.   _____
6. Jesus died, was buried, and rose from the dead.   _____
7. Jesus was born of a virgin.   _____
8. Jesus is coming again.   _____
9. The Holy Spirit is God.   _____
10. The Holy Spirit enters into a person when they believe. _____
11. The sign that a person has been filled with the Holy Spirit
    is speaking in tongues.   _____
12. If I'm good enough, I can go to heaven.   _____
13. If I repent of my sins and trust in Jesus for salvation,
    I will go to heaven.   _____
14. Once a person has put their faith in Jesus, heaven is
    a certain future for them.   _____
15. God exists as three separate persons – Father, Son (Jesus),
    and Holy Spirit – yet, He is one.   _____
16. It was necessary for Jesus to die on the cross.   _____
17. There is a real place called Hell.

18. Every human being is a sinner. _____
19. Infants should be baptized. _____
20. You cannot be saved without being baptized. _____